Every young Am...

It challenges e...

himself what ...

leave upon mankin...

George S. Brown
General, USAF
Chairman, Joint Chiefs of Staff

Col *[signature]*

COLONEL HEATH BOTTOMLY

PRODIGAL FATHER

A Fighter Pilot finds peace in the wake of his destruction

A Division of G/L Publications
Glendale, California, U.S.A.

Illustrated by Jim Lamb

Some of the photos in this book courtesy of Family Films, Hollywood, California, distributors of the film *The Conversion of Colonel Bottomly*.

The combat portions of this narrative have been modified sufficiently to comply with the National Security Act of 1948, thus protecting sensitive and classified military activities.

The foreign language publishing of all Regal books is under the direction of GLINT. GLINT provides financial and technical help for the adaptation, translation and publishing of books in more than 85 languages for millions of people worldwide.

For more information write: GLINT, P.O. Box 6688, Ventura, CA 93006.

Fourth printing, 1980

Published by Regal Books Division, G/L Publications
Glendale, California 91209
Printed in U.S.A.

Library of Congress Catalog Card No. 75-14884
ISBN 0-8307-0431-0

Dedicated

To my eldest son, Roc, who led me out of the darkness and into the light on the night of 31 October, 1969.

To my dearest friend, Lionel Mayell, who took me in out of the cold and taught me how to walk in the Spirit and how to share and grow. He handed down his ministry to me as a father to his son.

To my Betsy who has endured in love my thirty-year-long carnal drive for power B.C.—as well as the unpredictable slings and arrows of the past five years—through the torturous battles for control of my life between the old self and the Spirit of the living God.

To the Navigators and Campus Crusade for Christ who together, through His mysterious ways, led my whole family to God.

CONTENTS

foreword

I met Colonel Bottomly ten years ago when I came into the Pentagon to report to the Joint Chiefs of Staff on the findings of a task force I then commanded. But I really got to know him when I went to Saigon in 1968 to command the theater air forces in Southeast Asia. He was my Chief of Plans and Programs at Seventh Air Force as well as my noon-hour tennis partner.

Colonel Bottomly is a classic stencil of an American military professional. His thirty-three years in uniform spanned four wars including a World War II P-38 tour in the Southwest Pacific, Korea, a summer in Palestine observing the Arab-Israeli fighting and three tours in Southeast Asia. During the 1969-1970 campaign to interdict the enemy supplies along the Ho Chi Minh Trail and the Mekong River, he commanded all the F-105 fighter bombers in the war. His close work with my tactical staff brought a noticeable improvement in the effectiveness of this campaign. Colonel Bottomly was unusually ambitious, self reliant and innovative. Like most fighter pilots he was direct, earthy, often in some kind of hot water, but he was always in the arena. He was one of the best. He lived the legend of the friendly, maverick, fighting wing commander.

This story is really a sketchy autobiography of such a man. It shows how fighter pilots are created and shaped into a breed apart—how they are encouraged to develop initiative and self confidence. It also flags the critical need for strict air discipline in modern conflicts. Against this professional backdrop, the story sketches how warm and human most fighting men are inside—whether soldiers, sailors, marines or aviators. Even more important, it demonstrates how God can get hold of any man's heart.

I do not recall the details of the mission Bo threads through his parable of the prodigal father. But I am sure something of indelible significance of like nature happened at this time in his life because all of us around him could see his life changing course. I had great expectations of his rising to positions of very high responsibility calling for general officer rank, but obviously the Lord had other plans.

His new career as a full time soldier of God can be of great service in helping to turn our country around morally—to turn America back from a course of permissiveness and moral decay to a pursuit of excellence, a pursuit of high standards of integrity and purpose. We need this badly.

Every young American should read this book. It challenges each of us to decide for himself what mark, if any, his life will leave upon mankind after he has gone on.

George S. Brown
General, USAF
Chairman, Joint Chiefs of Staff

acknowledgments

My special thanks to Dr. Cyrus N. Nelson, President of the Greater Los Angeles Sunday School Association, who challenged me to put this parable down on paper and then kept after me until I had done so.

My thanks also to my editor and friend, Earl Roe, whose tireless work and helpful criticism is evident on every page of this book.

My warmest regards to General George S. Brown, the finest officer and gentleman I have ever known. As the years have passed, I have followed his rise to unusual influence with undiminished warmth. One cannot fret about our country's woes when men of such caliber are directing our nation's course.

My gratitude to Lieutenant General Ernest Hardin Jr., my last boss in the Air Force. He guided me through the last four years of my Air Force career and encouraged my Christian growth and ministry.

My heartfelt appreciation goes out as well to the hundreds of Christian friends in neighborhood churches, in college auditoriums, in retreats and camps and in seminaries who have encouraged me to keep after this undertaking by daily asking, "When is your book coming out?" You know who you are. God bless you.

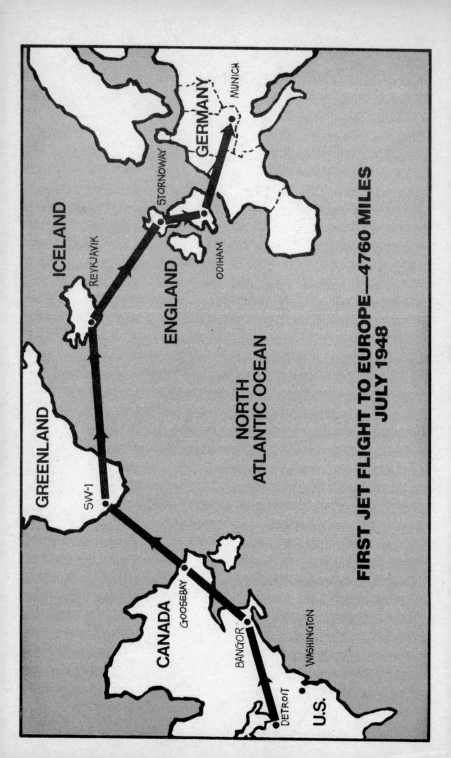

**FIRST JET FLIGHT TO EUROPE—4760 MILES
JULY 1948**

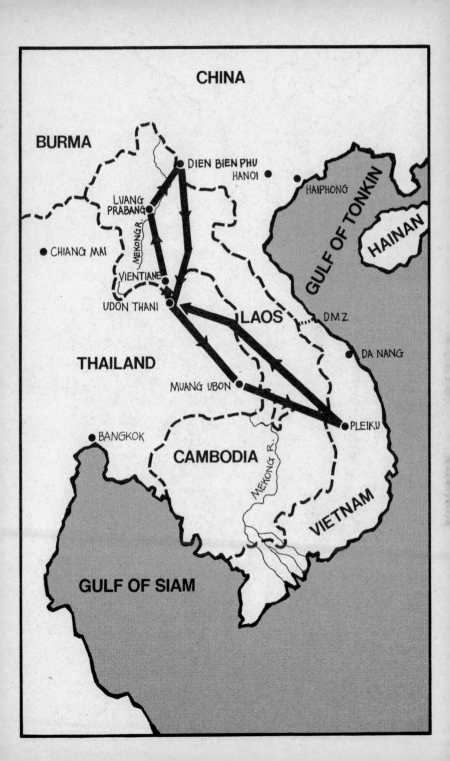

1
trying
to change
the world

Nothing, absolutely nothing, is as black as a predawn takeoff from a jungle fighter base in a relentless, drizzling, monsoon rain. Soft black sky. Glistening black earth. Glowing black cockpit.

The radio crackled in my jet helmet. "Dragon flight, this is Takhli tower. You're cleared on the runway."

"Roger, Takhli."

Without signaling the F-105s beside me, I eased up the throttle and felt my bomb-loaded fighter creep ahead in the dark. I swung a wide arc to the far side of the runway, leaving room for my three buddies to join me in takeoff position.

They swung their sleek fighters into echelon with mine—aligning canopies and glowing wing lights.

On the end of the runway we paused a moment. Through the blur, I could discern the flashing lights of the remaining flights marshaling on the taxiway behind us. All was on schedule at one minute past four, 29 October 1969 at Takhli Airbase in Thailand. This was a critical dawn interdiction strike against the Ho Chi Minh Trail in Laos.

I punched the mike button on the throttle and gingerly released it. That gesture put a single click in each wingman's ear—the signal for full power checkout.

Outside, the steady whine of contented engines gradually rose to a deafening, angry scream, as four green steel panthers crouched down to spring into the night. My instrument needles settled steady on the maximum power markers. I searched the pelting blur ahead. Two converging rows of dim, distorted cat's eyes ran out toward a black infinity. A trickle of sweat edged down my nose and dripped. I glanced down the mute formation. The radio silence meant all okay.

Three seconds. Two seconds. One second. My brain spat. "Release brakes! Light the afterburner!"

Flash! Bang! Behind me, a deafening, scarlet blast ripped the night wide open. My head snapped. Then, trailing a yard of fire, howling mad, throwing a wake of spray, I plunged forward into the black beyond—completely consumed by that mix of emotions all adventurers feel at the moment of truth—stark terror and utter exhilaration.

Softly and quietly up from the far-off recesses of my memory floated images of similar mixes of terror and transcending joy. My youth was a chain of such experiences. I was one of seven sons of a father with great expectations and a mother with an incredible reservoir of love and patience.

To raise up his seven sons, my father—a tough Montana pioneer lawyer—chose strict discipline and a code of simple rules. He and Mother were determined that we all would survive, would develop the skills needed to overcome any adversity and would achieve the education necessary to climb ahead—each in his own way—in a steady, sensible progression to honest, worthy success in life.

Dad revered the simple, honest, straight way. He concentrated on the basics. He taught us to be independent and self-reliant, to develop skills, to learn to improvise, to stand on our own two feet—not to borrow, not to lend, not to lean, not to cry for help.

Dad taught us persistence and determination. Nothing brought down his wrath like a quitter, except perhaps a liar. He taught us will power—the greatest source of abstract strength in the universe.

Furthermore, he taught us pride—pride in what a lad could do with just what he had within him—skill, will, perseverance and lots of enthusiasm. He taught us to be proud of ourselves and of each other. And he was proud of us, both individually and collectively.

One of those delicious other moments of terror and exhilaration occurred when I was nine years old. It was August, 1928. Dad packed the family into our old Dodge, and we headed for the mountains on a great adventure. We drove west from the little Montana cattle town of Chinook, our hometown. All day we rumbled west across the plains and up into the foothills. At dusk we arrived at Glacier Park and camped.

The next morning we drove on up through the mighty Rockies. Near the timberline the road stopped. We loaded our gear on our backs and hiked the trail up through the great, gray, granite crags. Finally we unloaded in the shadow of the highest peak around and pitched our camp.

In the morning we climbed on. Up, up, up, we went to where a great blue-white glacier lay against the northern slope of this spectacular crag. There, even in August, ice hundreds of feet deep defied the summer sun. Gasping for breath and stunned by the view, we stood on top of the world and looked out over four states and into Canada.

Down the glacier's face, cutting a narrow ditch, plunged the icy water of the melt. Past our feet this little stream raced in a noisy shout—out across a flat plate of rock. Gathering speed it shot into space, hung there a moment, and then tumbled thousands of feet toward the valley below.

We inched forward to the edge, and as Dad shouted and pointed, we could see the water split below. Some slid off to the west and crashed down on the great stone shoulder of the mountain, disintegrated into spray showering the laurel and alder bushes, and then trickled from stream to lake toward the Middle Fork of the Flathead River that feeds the mighty Columbia and dumps into the Pacific Ocean.

A central segment of the stream pitched straight ahead to the north and fanned out into a turkey tail of rainbow colors. It drifted in slow motion down, down into the canopy of giant cedars, spruce and fir and fell out of sight into the valley whose waters fed the Mackenzie and Yukon rivers and ultimately found its way to the Arctic Ocean. Over to the right—to the east—the stream smashed between two towering rocks and plunged unobstructed thousands of feet through space to flash on the mossy rock-covered shore of beautiful St. Mary's Lake—the headwaters of the Milk River, which dumps into the Missouri, which feeds the Mississippi, which winds its way into the Atlantic Ocean.

Spellbound we watched this incredible drama as Dad edged forward onto the flat rock—out to where the icy stream plunged into space. Opening his fingers, he put his hand into the water. I could see from where I crouched with my brothers that as his hand moved, the water pattern changed accordingly.

After a moment, Dad signaled us away from the edge of eternity—away from the boisterous laughter of the stream—up onto a grassy knoll. He pointed to the peak soaring above us. "Boys, this is the top of the world. This is where the seas are born. The water you just watched running through my fingers will soon be part of the tides in the great oceans that surround our land."

It was an awesome moment. We all breathed a little deeper than we ever had before.

Dad beckoned and the boys fell into file and, like a band of tiny Indians, snaked down the trail toward camp. It would soon be time for lunch. But I did not follow. An unusual stir twisted my stomach and held me to the knoll. There was more here.

I watched the little column turn the corner and disappear. I ran to the flat, stone slab where Dad had stood. I crept forward to the very edge. There I plunged my left hand into the rushing stream as it hung in the air. It was ice cold.

With all my strength I pushed the stream over to the left. With my flat palm and wrist aching, I pressed the water over to the west and changed its course. I held it there though it fought and burned and ached. I gritted my teeth and pushed it hard.

Suddenly, I felt a tug on my sweater. Turning, I faced Dad, who had missed me on the trail and returned. As I stepped back from the edge, he swept me up into his great arms and turned toward the trail. As we rounded the ledge and the shouting stream was gone, he put me down. But he didn't let me go.

He squatted down and looked directly into my face. "Son, I'm proud of you. You're nine years old and already you're trying to change the world. I watched you. That water was going into the Atlantic Ocean and you deliberately pushed it into the Pacific."

He put his hand on my shoulder, and we hustled on to catch the rest of the gang.

My soul was on fire. My thoughts raced. "What power man has! With one hand I can change the face of the earth. From now on the Atlantic will be a little shallower—and the Pacific, a little deeper."

Much of the chain of my youth ran through those fabulous mountains of Glacier Park. Four years later, Dad had erected a rough ranger cabin on the shore of Lake McDonald, and we began spending our summers there. During the long summer twilights, Mom and Dad would sit around the fire in the cabin and talk with neighbors, but we boys would toss our blankets on the beach and roll up to sleep under the canopy of stars.

One warm, quiet night I was just drifting off to sleep when I heard footfalls padding along the sand and then felt something flop down on the foot of my bedroll. I peeked out and there, silhouetted against the evening sky lay a large black bear. He had come down to the lake for supper and lay watching the surface of the water for signs of a fat trout or salmon—completely oblivious of the blanket rolls scattered about him on the sand.

I was not unusually upset until I saw him yawn. The sight of that great mouth filled with teeth stirred me into action. In one leap I was out of my blanket. Two bounds later, I was on the steps to the cabin. Dad loved to watch the dusk settle over the lake and he was standing in the screen door as I ran through it. He sort of fielded me like a fast grounder and lifted me off the deck.

"Hey, what's going on here?"

"A . . . a . . . a big grizzly is down there trying to share my bed, so I decided to come share yours."

"What d'ya mean? It's your bed, isn't it? He's got no right to it. You go back down there and chase him off."

I knew Dad wasn't kidding, so I hiked up my pajama bottoms and headed silently down the trail to the water. En route I selected several large stones from the border of the path. At the foot of the giant birch tree at the edge of the beach, I paused and took a deep breath—then with a wild Comanche scream, I leaped out onto the sand throwing stones like an artillery barrage and kicking sand at the big, black shape. The startled bear let out a muffled grunt and bounded away into the shadows.

I was very proud of my successful counterattack. Without so much as awakening my brothers, I scootched back down into my sleeping bag as cool as a cat and, in three or four hours, was fast asleep.

When dawn broke, Dad came down to wash his face in the lake, and remembering the little play of the night before, he meandered over to where I was curled up. He tickled me with his toe and when I opened my eyes, he was sitting astraddle me, smiling down. He let out an old cavalry reveille shout and in a minute all the boys were writhing awake. Knowing that where Dad was, the action was, they gathered around by rolling over and over in their warm blankets.

After rubbing or thumping each one, Dad began a wake-up story. "Boys, last night your brother here had some fun with a friendly bear who was snooping around the camp. He chased him off with his bare hands, and I'm proud of him. He showed a lot of cool."

There was a long pause. Six pairs of large eyes looked at me with wonder. I could feel the hot blood of pride and joy race in my veins as Dad began one of his many Jim Bridger stories—tales centered on a legendary frontier character who had been his childhood idol.

"Let me tell you lads about a youngster I used to know who was born cool. His name was Jim Bridger. When the Bridger family came west out of Kansas City, they followed the Oregon Trail by covered wagon up across the Dakotas. They forded the Yellowstone River in late summer and by October were camped on the Madison near Three Forks.

"A band of Blackfoot Indians caught 14-year-old Jim and his dad fishing in their river. They burned the wagon and massacred the entire family except for Jim—who was just your brother's age."

He thumped my chest. Big eyes again all around—spellbound and jealous.

"They bound young Jim in rawhide thongs and set up the vicious, savage, *gauntlet* for entertainment. The gauntlet was a wild, killing sport. The braves lined up in two long columns about five feet apart. They were armed with clubs, knives, tomahawks, spikes, trip thongs. The victim was stripped naked and barefoot. On signal, he was shoved into this slashing, tripping, beating, ripping, twisting avenue of yelling, laughing Indians.

"Normally, as the victim raced and fought his way along, he was scalped, skinned, chopped, bludgeoned and stabbed to screaming, bloody death—often disemboweled and dismembered while still fighting and screaming and running for life. No one had ever survived a Blackfoot gauntlet run.

"An hour before sunset young Jim stood looking down between two rows of armed and painted young devils. He was naked and cold and terrified beyond imagination—but loose as a cornered mountain lion. When the eagle screamed, Jim didn't wait to be shoved off balance.

"He leaped at the short, sharp knife in the lead brave's fist. A wrist twist and the blade fell free. He snatched it out of the air, bounced on to the one-armed giant diagonally across and ripped his groin open.

"Ducking low, he flashed past ten men, cutting two trip thongs as he flew. A club bit into his shoulder, a bowie knife opened his back. He guarded his legs and leapt and spun. He slashed the throat of a painted tiger, split the shins of a leering buffalo, sliced the thighs of a howling wolf.

"Up and down—bobbing, weaving, attacking, parrying, yelling, running, young Jim ricocheted through the tunnel of hell. Then with an unearthly scream of pain and defiance, he leapt from the open end of the gauntlet and raced for the river. Fifty angry, astonished, shouting braves followed at full tilt.

"A light snow crusted the gravelly turf where Jim raced out of the woods across a cactus and sagebrush flat—up along a sharp, shale ledge, through a poison briar tangle out onto the cliff overlooking the ice-glazed river. Arrows flashed by; lances whistled overhead; an angry mob howled on his heels.

"Jim ran the high cliff for a mile trying to outdistance his pursuers. Lungs bursting, heart pounding, body bleeding, muscles aching, he began losing ground. At the top of a rise, the lead brave touched Jim's heels in a flying tackle. That was close enough.

"Running full speed, the slender sprinter sprang in a long arc out over the river—then dropped like a falling shard. With a sharp crack, he pierced the thin ice leaving a tiny black hole in the smooth white glaze.

"He swam a quarter of a mile under the ice to the crest of the great falls. Over and down he plunged—five hundred feet into the churning pool below. Back under the falls he surfaced for air, glanced carefully around, scrambled ashore and melted into the yellow and scarlet forest."

Dad's eyes twinkled with warm pride as he searched each son's awestruck face. Then he very sharply slapped my bottom, stood up and said, "Boys, that's what I call cool. Come on, wash your faces and let's eat."

He turned and disappeared up the path toward the strong aroma of sizzling bacon.

2
i will!
i will!
i will!

Up, up and away! Gear up. The airspeed tape crept slowly toward 250 knots. Flaps up. Inky black lay ahead as the cat's eyes disappear below and behind. The rain on the canopy sounded like shrapnel; 350 knots—afterburner out. I leaned into a gradual left turn.

Suddenly into the clear air above the clouds. Silence and a million stars! A new moon knifed the eastern sky. Orion blazed. Spine tingled. Chest heaved. A spontaneous smile.

The radio crackled. "Dragon lead from Takhli tower. All off okay. You're cleared tower frequency. Squawk mode two, code zero four."

I squeezed the mike button. "Roger. Dragons, channel three. Channel three, go."

On radio channel three, the flight checked in and my peripheral vision picked up the blinking wing tip lights of "Number Four" as he slid into formation completing the join up. What precision. What timing. A thrill of pride swept my spine and formed into a thought.

"What an incredible adventure it is to be a combat wing commander. Way out here in the jungle wilderness of Thailand, you are really the modern version of the legendary Asian war lord. You have all the power—the majesty. You rule the great war base—the fortifications, the shops, the offices, the barracks. You design the tactics. You are responsible for the bombs, the guns—how they are stored and loaded and used. You are responsible for the crews on the ground—the pilots in the air. You are responsible for every man's mental attitude, his actions, his growth and, yes, even what he will become—his ultimate service to his country.

"This is the very crest of personal pride and power and responsibility in combat flying. But of equal significance is another facet of this challenge: your life is daily on the line. With all of this power and accountability and trust, as a combat wing commander, you are out there leading the force and being shot at in anger by a well-trained, deadly serious enemy, every day of your life."

Few living human beings ever get to experience this incredibly terrifying, exhilarating view from the crest. It evades the grasp of even most air generals, many of whom have told me personally that they would gladly trade their stars for a year as a combat wing commander.

Nonetheless such a unique thrill is always transitory in an ambitious man's climb. I recalled in a fleeting second my beloved General George S. Brown's quizzical look in his great office on Tan Son Nuit Air Base in Saigon the day he sent me to this great combat command. I had thanked him for his confidence in me and for this unusual opportunity.

Then I had asked, "General, tell me, how much power and glory is sufficient to satisfy a man's ambition in this life?"

He looked me straight in the eye and replied, "Just a little more."

This will to power. This instinctive drive for the very top had grown out of the tap roots of Dad's old disciplined code of persistence, pride and contagious enthusiasm—together with Mom's steadfast loyalty to him. I never heard one word of contention between my parents in my twenty years at home. They held to a single philosophy on bringing up boys, and they lived by it all the way.

From that straight-willow childhood in Chinook, my tree of life grew as naturally and predictably as any redwood in the forest. But one strange, enigmatic incident came close to bending that tree of mine in a new direction. I was perhaps eleven years old at the time. My big brother was two years older.

One crisp September evening we had donned our heavy home-knit sweaters and escaped into the drawing dusk out our bedroom window. We were allegedly studying our homework, while below in a warm, joyous atmosphere Mom was singing at the piano. We slipped down the porch shingles and dropped to the turf. Then across the garden and over the back hedge into the alley. We were free and off once again on another spine-tingling adventure—stealing crabapples.

I followed brother Vic's shadow as it darted along the

neighbor's picket fence and flattened out across Leonard's cabbage patch. The cold autumn moon frosted the stubble of Arnold's vacant lot across the street. Our sneakers sped us silently as ghosts up the alley to the huge apple tree behind Canfields' house. We ducked down behind the high board fence to catch our breath.

Peeking between cracks we cased the backyard. All was serene—warm lights within—young Alice practicing her flute. Employing Boy Scout wall scaling techniques I boosted Vic over and was pulled after him. The ground under the tree was rich with crabapples. We loaded our sweater pockets and, as I paused to take a bite from an especially large specimen, Canfields' back screen door sprang open and Mr. Canfield, our friendly local grocer, leveled a shotgun loaded with salt pellets.

"All right, boys. Hold it right there."

Discarding accepted procedure, my brother and I simultaneously vaulted the seven-foot fence. The night exploded with the loudest bang I have ever heard, and voices seemed to erupt from door yards everywhere. We flashed down the alley, cut between two houses and turned north across the street. There we ducked behind the giant lilac bushes hiding Stams' garbage cans.

We waited. From somewhere came the low moan of the town marshal's siren mounted on his Model A Ford.

We panicked. Sweater tails flying, we raced down the sidewalk for two blocks and turned to follow the dirt path cutting across the vacant lot next to the Methodist church. It was not vacant tonight.

Providence had provided the ultimate sanctuary—a huge canvas tent. We leapt the low sign announcing a week-long Billy Sunday Revival and darted under the tent flap. The back row of wooden benches was empty. We each grabbed a hymnbook and joined "Bringing in the Sheaves" as the audience started the second verse.

We heard the posse pass outside as we huddled together listening to one of the world's most colorful evangelists lash out against sin. And Billy's message got right through to my soul.

Finally the altar call came. I knew God could see my sweater pockets bulging with sin, and I wanted to be saved. I leaned against my brother and whispered, "Vic, let's go down and get forgiven. If God's with us, the marshal won't bother us, and Mom will never be the wiser."

"Are you kidding?" my brother exploded. "With all these stolen apples? They'd stick us in the pokey and trot us into Dad in the morning."

Dad was County Attorney at the time.

"You're right," I answered. "We'd look pretty bad unloading our loot at Billy Sunday's feet."

And so like ships that pass in the night, my young life brushed close to a different world. I felt the current and paused, but then inertia swept it on its course.

As I guided my formation steadily toward its target in eastern Laos, I tried to think of how that inertia really started. The radar of my mind swept back over the years and picked up a couple of telltale blips far back. Then as the cursor swept again and again, a vector formed from two tiny, far-off incidents that seemed almost mundane at the time. One came in my seventh autumn. The other happened later that same winter.

Many times as a lad I rode horseback south from the suburbs

of Chinook, Montana toward the Bear Paw Mountains, twenty-five miles away. A mile south of town we crossed the river and climbed up through the hills until we came out onto a great, open prairie where wild flowers danced in the sun as far as the eye could see.

Fifteen miles out along that old wagon road, I would pull up my horse and gaze down a steep, grassy hill to a tiny creek below. Often I imagined I could still hear that valley and the hills beyond echo with the sound of shot and shell and smell the acrid powder smoke of a very cold October day in 1877—the last great Indian battle in the opening of the west.

As dusk fell on that bitter day, Chief Joseph of the Nez Perce nation walked up the south promontory commanding the valley and handed his Winchester to General Nelson A. Miles. The old chief pointed to the west and said, "From where the sun now stands, I will fight no more, forever!"

One of my very earliest memories—I was just seven then—is of that valley and those hills. Every year in October the people from all around gather on that battlefield to commemorate the peace that still reigns across those Montana plains. By noon on Surrender Day each year, the hillsides and the valley are dotted with picnic baskets and colorful tablecloths spread out on the prairie grass or under the cottonwood trees.

At one o'clock the crowd gathers up on the promontory where a stone monument is erected to mark the surrender site. And there some distinguished western statesman addresses the crowd. It is a festive day—sort of an autumn Fourth of July.

On this day I remember, all the great figures of the day had sent their regrets. Senator Borah of Idaho as well as Montana's Senators Burton K. Wheeler and Tom Walsh—all were busy in the Capitol. As a last frantic measure the committee asked my father to speak. He was overjoyed. He was running for County Attorney against a strong Republican incumbent; this invitation a month before election day was a stroke of providence.

I can see him now, standing there beside the great monument, his frock coat blowing in the wind. Before him on the prairie carpet, a captive audience of thousands who had come from far and near expecting to hear one of the nation's great. On the left in their big Montana stetsons, sat the cattlemen. On the right, in their familiar bib overalls, were the sheepmen. And in between, keeping the peace—the Indians.

Dad's message was simple. He had no favorites. If elected, he would pay equal attention to the bribes of the wealthy cattlemen, the threats of the sullen sheepmen and the anguished cries of the maligned and neglected Indians.

In his concluding lines from William E. Henley's *Invictus,* he was superb. I can hear Dad's voice to this day—rising over the ceaseless prairie wind.

"It matters not how straight the gate
How charged with punishment the scroll,
For I am the master of my fate
I am the captain of my soul."

The crowd was on its feet in a standing ovation. Hats were thrown in the air. With tears in his eyes, old Chief Bearfoot, grandson of Joseph, walked forward to shake Dad's hand and—in a gesture of unusual warmth and sheer political genius—Dad took off his frock coat and draped it over those hunched old shoulders.

Ten yards to one side, sitting in the tall grass surrounding their mother were the speaker's five sons—eyes sparkling, mouths open in awe, chests pounding with pride. A fire storm swept my seven-year-old soul. Mother says that I stood up at that point and walked to where she sat. Eyes on a level with her own, I said deliberately and seriously, "When I grow up, I'm going to be captain of my soul, too!"

Then I walked back and sat down.

Curiously enough, it was on this same road out of town—though not quite as far south as the battlefield—that our winter caper took place three months later. It happened on a magnificent Montana Sunday in early January. Dawn had come up that day like a burst of fireworks—crisp and clear and golden. And the snow lay deep and cold like a blanket of powdered diamonds.

We loaded our new Christmas skis onto the old Dodge. Then all piled in, and we headed for the hills beyond the river, our tire chains ringing a sleighbell chant. Five miles south beyond the river, we stopped.

Hill after hill, we shot; we raced; we tumbled; we laughed. By late afternoon we were cold and wet and hungry and reluctantly decided to call it a day—the end of a day of utter joy outdoors.

Sometime every winter a savage blizzard builds up in Western Canada. Then without warning it spills over the Rocky Mountains and sweeps east across the Montana prairie like a great, white ghost.

It took only a few minutes for the final "one last" sally down the steep slope, kick off skis, laugh and shout to one another and plod back to the car. From the top of the hill to where the car was parked was perhaps 400 yards, but that quarter mile turned suddenly into an impenetrable wall of blinding, biting snow driven by a hurricane-force wind.

Dad pulled us all together and shouting encouragement to one another, we tramped to the car. Only a few minutes had lapsed, but already the snow was drifting. The car was almost submerged. No way would we get home but on foot. We left our skis and, in single file behind Dad, leaned against the wind toward home five miles away. In heavy overshoes, sodden, frozen mittens, knit sweaters buttoned chin tight, scarves wrapped across our faces, we waded through waist-high drifts.

On a direct line, into the face of the storm, we trudged on, chanting above the williwaw, "I will! I will! I will!" Three hours later, out of the icy blackness of the winter night, completely spent and leaning on one another for strength with Dad carrying the youngest, but still chanting, we fell into Mom's warm kitchen.

We were exhausted, but elated.

We had overcome!

We had survived!

8
riding
the wind

I spread the formation out and gave the guys a chance to relax a bit as we swept north in the night. A combat takeoff at maximum load with lots of afterburner time consumes a lot of fuel, so our first task was to rendezvous with the great silver tankers awaiting us in orbit to the north along the Mekong River.

Below us in the dark, the green jungle and the irregular peaks of the karst mountains slid south under our bellies. Above us spread a hemisphere of sapphires. Now was the time to relax and, as I did so, my mind went back once again to my youth.

As my high school years flew by, it was a natural outgrowth of my taproots of persistence, self-reliance and enthusiasm for me to begin noticing man as a singular phenomenon. I became aware of man's amazing strength and versatility. I saw how little awed he is by the dimensions of his universe, how undismayed by the complexity of his problems, how unterrified by the fragility of his existence.

I viewed man as challenged, rather than deterred, by adversity. He has charged forth to explore his globe and encircled it with ribbons of steel and concrete. He has come to the waters and spanned them with girders and cables and ships.

He has come up against the sky, and fashioning wings has leapt into the heavens. He has shot shards of glass and steel and aluminum into space and has learned to live aloft. He has noticed the stars and dreams now of conquering and developing the universe.

When the time came, it seemed a natural step for me to escape that little Montana cattle town and go east to West Point to study conflict. And there, it was just as natural in my progression that I should be drawn to the dynamic humanistic philosophy then current in the great colleges and universities of the east.

In the mid-1940s, everyone was reading and listening to Bertrand Russell, Friedrich Nietzsche, Eric Fromm and Ayn Rand. A bold, masculine philosophy was abroad. Its main thrust: man is the center of the universe. Alone as a significant, reasoning entity, he creates gods in his own image to meet his own drives and needs.

Rejecting supernaturalism, this dynamic humanistic philosophy holds that man is totally responsible for what he is and what he becomes, and for developing the meaning of his existence. He alone is accountable for the conduct of nations, for the achievements of mankind and for the rise and fall of civilization as it undulates out across eternity. Man is the total master of his fate, including mastery over the "immutable laws" of nature. In the man equation, there is no supernatural power involved.

This was an exciting metaphysic among us twenty-year-olds. We read it avidly, listened to its prophets, discussed its merits. Moreover we couldn't wait to get out of those ivy-covered, greystone walls and practice this concept in real life. This dynamic human theme meant that what we made of our lives depended entirely upon ourselves—our skills, our determination, our will power.

I remembered sitting on a simple stone bench on the plain at West Point a few days before graduation. I noted that the time was fast approaching when I would explode out of those four grey walls into the real world. I rejoiced in anticipation of setting the world on fire.

That day as I gazed up the Hudson River and dreamed of leading space armadas out to colonize and police the planets, I swore an oath to myself. I promised myself that I would live by this dynamic, driving, humanistic philosophy—never diluting or polluting it—and see if I could climb to the top alone with just what I had within me.

My graduation came when America was in the middle of World War II. I was sent almost immediately to the Southwest Pacific theater as a P-38 pilot. Our task out there was to help sweep the skies of enemy aircraft and search out where the enemy was and what he was doing. I loved the life of a fighter pilot. The P-38 fit right into my metaphysic and my life-style: one man—one airplane.

A fighter pilot lived or died in the high thin air over the vast Pacific according to how well he had developed his skills as a flier and the guts he could muster when he was one-on-one against an enemy Zero—the will power he could bring to bear in that moment of truth when he is all alone out there in the sky with one engine dead and home base a thousand miles away.

We proved to be very successful in our mission to clear the skies. We skipped north from island to island, from New Guinea to the Halmaheras to the Philippines. And we chased the enemy back and back until he retreated to his air bases on the China coast and the offshore islands.

Then suddenly we found that we had fought ourselves out of the war—at least temporarily. We had pushed the enemy back so far, we could no longer reach him from our island bases with our little fighters. Our small craft simply didn't have the range to make longer forays. We chafed at being out of combat now, but we were not long in awaiting action.

The theater commander saw our plight and sent us an expert aeronautical engineer to help us extend the range of our fighters. He was a tall, thin, smiling civilian scientist in a grey, Navy flying suit that was much too small—the trouser legs didn't reach even to his ankles. I knew I was going to like this man, and our friendship started that very first day.

He walked up to our commander's tent on the beach and introduced himself. He said, "Major, I think I can help you. We've been doing some range extending with the 475th Fighter Group. I'd like to fly a few days of tests on your model. I feel confident that we can stretch out your range and get you back into the war.

"One thing I'd like to ask. I'll need one of your best, all-round pilots to work with me. You know, if I disappear out over the Pacific, you'll never know what I did wrong."

"Of course," our commander replied, looking out over the white sandy beach nearby where a full quota of young American manhood was playing volleyball—naked. There were no women on the island and, as temperatures often reached 135 degrees at noon, we usually played volleyball in the buff.

So there we were, without a stitch of clothes on. And as the commander stood there looking us over and reflecting, a mighty roar caught his attention. Across the surf at blinding speed flashed a lone, Japanese Betty bomber.

In an instant the beach and adjacent fighter pads were a wild, yelling melee of naked bodies as 50 fighter pilots streaked for their aircraft. Everyone wanted to be the hero who would shoot down the intruder.

A few scattered explosions erupted as bombs cratered the ramp. Allison engines belched blue smoke, crew chiefs yelled signals, propellers whirled and a silver stream of P-38s roared off across the horizon at wavetop level, guns blazing away at that poor lonely bomber.

Soon the fun was over and, gathering in formation, we headed back for home. But fortune had other plans in store for us that day. While we were chasing the enemy bomber across the horizon, a great thunderstorm rolled out of the east. It paused right over our island and poured down rain and hail for eight hours—and we had to go land at another base.

Somewhere a lonely tower operator sat quietly in his little greenhouse, alternately dozing and reading a dog-eared comic book. Without warning, the sky above him exploded with P-38s peeling off and circling to land. They taxied in and lined up before him on the ramp, wingtip to wingtip. Wall-to-wall P-38s! Then someone gave a signal and 50 naked pilots leaped from their aircraft and raced for cover in the jungle.

The next day we were back at home base, the laughing stock of the islands. It was then that the commander called me in and told me that I was to work with the new guy for a few days. I soon found out what this meant, and—since I was just a second lieutenant with only six months in the theater—I was thrilled to be selected over all those majors, captains and first lieutenants.

As I reflected on what my buddies called my "good luck," I thought, "You see, you are already standing out in this crowd because of your will power philosophy. These guys are all wanderers on the earth. They don't have any goals—any philosophy of life, but you do. You know where you are headed. One of these days, you'll run this whole outfit."

For 10 days, the skinny engineer and I flew all sorts of cruise control missions. We leaned out the mixture until we were burning mostly air. We pulled back the RPM on those Allison engines until you could count the propeller blades turning. We pushed the manifold pressure up until we cracked the cylinder heads.

Finally on the eleventh day, before dawn we loaded about a thousand gallons of 115-octane gasoline into two of our latest model P-38s. Then just as the eastern sky turned red, we flushed and headed for China. Out across the Pacific, we climbed and climbed and climbed.

Now I found myself being woven into one of those curious and delightful real, yet unreal, true-life stories. I felt as though I were a character apart from life, living out a role in a historic novel.

Soon I could see the coastline of Asia creeping in under my nose. I could identify Hong Kong and Kowloon. Inland a few miles, Canton rested astride the mighty Yu Si River flowing yellow out of the Asian hinterland.

My head throbbed with excitement. I'd never seen these

places before except on maps. And now here I was, a latter-day Marco Polo flying into war-torn China to explore, to fight, to liberate. I became so absorbed with the thought that I was here living on the edge of history that I momentarily forgot my checklist.

Suddenly I came awake. Next item: "check your fuel." I glanced at the fuel gauge in shock. Two hundred gallons! I made a quick calculation. We broke ground with 1000 gallons. Now we were just halfway, and I showed only 200 gallons. Something had gone radically wrong!

I tried to signal the leader by rocking my wings, but he was busily photographing the military installations down on the China coast and paying no attention to my gyrations. Finally, as I was about to blow a gasket, he bent us around and headed east for home.

Now we were very light, so we drifted higher and higher as we reduced the RPM and inched up the manifold pressure. We were so high, I could hardly breathe—even on full oxygen. Still we climbed higher. And higher. In fact, that day—I'm told—we flew those two P-38s higher than man had ever flown a fighter plane before.

At those great heights we discovered a phenomenon most of us pilots weren't yet familiar with. At that very low latitude near the equator and that very high altitude, a band of air rushes around the earth from west to east at over 200 miles an hour. We joined this wind band and rode it out across the Pacific. It was like riding a tight wire across the heavens—teetering from side to side, almost falling out of the sky.

When we leveled off, my gauge read 50 gallons. And before me there was nothing but flat Pacific as far as the eye could reach. My spine tingled as I noticed for the first time in my life the thin, black line of the earth's curvature where the horizon fell away to north and south.

After an hour, a fine chalk line appeared on the horizon—the surf breaking on our beach. I showed 10 gallons. We pulled all the power off to idle and glided—floated—down, down, down. Time stood still as, silent as seagulls, we swished in across the surf.

My fuel needle showed flat empty. It was stuck over in the left corner of the instrument hard against the peg. I bit my lip awaiting an engine cough. None came.

In that timeless moment, the training of my youth prodded my mind. "I will. I will. I will!"

Our engineer broke radio silence to tell the tower to clear the runway; we were coming straight in from the west. I touched down 50 yards behind him and, on touchdown, both my propellers stopped turning. As we coasted down the runway and braked to a stop, I noticed that my leader's engines also stood dead.

He ran down the left boom and jumped to the ground, sporting a wide grin. He came over and pounded on the aluminum side of my cockpit. I threw open the hatch and was about to explode with a volley of epithets. But something about the man stopped me. His tousled greying hair was wet, and his smile wove crinkles around his eyes.

"See, Buddy," he said. "I told you we could make it." His voice was so casual and reassuring, I forgot my angry retort and began to laugh almost hysterically. Shouting, cheering fighter pilots surrounded us, pounding us on the back and shaking our hands. Some opened tall bottles of Aussie beer and poured it over us in celebration. We had broken some kind of world record.

The next few days were a flurry of training. By the end of the week we had written down the procedures and had taught every pilot on the island how to fly to China. By the end of the month we were averaging 50 combat missions a day—driving the enemy up the coast back toward his home islands.

For me, a young lieutenant, to participate like this in a major breakthrough for our fighter wing was an incredible thrill. Still I held my own counsel and said to myself, "See, you are holding true to your metaphysic, and it is paying off as advertised. One of these days, you will be running this whole Air Corps—maybe even more."

It never crossed my mind during these young, driving, stallion years that I was not destined to cut a mark of great significance across the face of mankind!

Still, more stimulating than anything else, even more powerful in impact, even more ego-building, even more clearly a validation of my existential philosophy than breaking open the fighter war for our islands, was living in the same tent, eating at the same mess bench, talking and laughing and flying with that tall, quiet engineer, Charles A. Lindbergh.

4
the women in my life

Anywhere on earth, watching dawn's victory over night is an absolutely absorbing sight. Still, southern Asia, during the monsoon season, manages to accompany the dawn with a soul-tingling splendor all its own. And this day as we winged our way toward our target in Laos, I saw and felt dawn's glories anew. The explosion of scarlet and gold in the towering clouds over the South China Sea reflected off the glass canopy of my wingman far out to the left.

The sudden coming of day brought me back to the present. Off to the right my element of two green and brown mottled fighters flashed against the blazing sky. They raced along in perfect position a thousand yards off my wing. I switched the flight to tanker frequency as, below us, we glimpsed the dark snake called the Mekong River lashing its tail west toward Vientiane.

Midair refueling is, next to dive-bombing the target, the most exciting and demanding part of a combat mission—especially when a pilot is low on fuel and he's got to get hooked up or fall out of the sky. I've watched some of my coolest-headed leaders choke up in spastic panic as they try to ease gently into position behind a bouncing tanker, rushing in and out of clouds at 350 knots. Moment after agonizing moment they watch their fast-fading fuel supply burn down to nothing on the gauge, the hair standing out straight on neck and arms, as they await the sudden silence of the flameout that could mean Hanoi prison or sudden death.

But while they wait, these men calmly, deliberately take an inner grip on the very roots of their souls and relax as, with fantastic precision, they squeeze the controls and thread that needle in the sky. Fuel comes flowing through and there is no sudden silence.

These are real soul-testing seconds, blood-curdling experiences that are not uncommon to fighter pilots, yet rarely befall other normal human beings. It is a whole bundle of such encounters that, day after incredible day, slowly turns fighter pilots into a breed apart.

This morning, however, there was no such sweat. The flight closed in as we spotted the tanker's blinking lights against the paling sky. We held a thousand feet below him and gently, steadily overtook the huge silver fish in a lazy port turn. Up close, the refueling boom lashed back and forth.

I killed our overtake speed by climbing the last thousand feet to the tanker's tail. My flight eased away from me into position, flying formation on the mother ship. She held steady as a rock. I gulped 4000 pounds from the pencil breast and felt my strength revive—my muscles relax.

I thought, "It's an amazing love affair—the fighters and the tankers. It's the simplest have-and-need, love-and-trust relationship this side of mother and child."

Almost unconsciously, I remembered a few of these absolutely simple, basic, have-and-need moments in my early life. One really stood out in solitary beauty as a tiny, mighty symbol of mother-son relationships.

One of the large events in every person's life is his first day in school. I remember I approached the day with mixed emotions. My big brother had teased me with wild stories of ruler slaps and standing-in-the-corner. Mom had tried to build my confidence with low-key comments on how sweet and helpful was Miss Hoole, the teacher. As life usually turns out, my first day was a little of each.

The day was a whirlwind of activity through which, at every turn, the warm, round face of Miss Hoole owled down at me and said quietly, but emphatically, "Put the pencil in your other hand, dear."

I ran all the way home after class was out and burst through the front door throwing myself into Mom's great skirt in a cloudburst of tears.

"Why am I left-handed?"

As she did with every unexpected disaster presented to her by her several sons, Mom reacted consistently and coolly to this one. She swept me up, buried my face in her ample bosom and brought me down in her lap on the couch. She mopped my face with her flowered apron.

"There, there, there, my son," she soothed. "The world is

made of people who write and draw and throw with their right hands. You have been picked out special. God has chosen you to do something very unusual for Him. To do this special thing, He has made you different from the others. Miss Hoole didn't know that. I'll tell her. Everything will be all right."

I raised up my head and looked into the biggest, warmest hazel eyes I have ever seen. There was no doubt in those eyes.

"Honest, Mom?"

"Honest, Son. Wait and see."

I was completely renewed—baptized with love and trust. Never would I have believed then that one day a giant lumbering, SAC fuel tanker would remind me of Mother. But it did. The utter need and the simple, complete fulfillment.

Full of fuel again and exactly on time, the flight held formation and climbed toward Mu Ghia Pass. It was a time to relax and rest and think. This could be a great day.

I mean really great.

If we could close the pass at Mu Ghia completely so that it could not be opened until the monsoon died, we could change the whole course of the war. It could be a new crest. It could mean Silver Star medals for many—perhaps the Air Force Cross for one or two.

I would then be called back to the White House. How proud my wife would be. Come to think of it, where would Betty be now? I wondered if she were still in the Washington area.

It had been so long since Betty or I had written. There

seems so little time in war to write or even think of wives. But even so I never worry about Betty. She's self-sufficient and doesn't need a lot of attention. She lives a full life.

It was sort of the same when we first met in the middle of World War II. From the beginning, Betty and I were very much alike: two strong lives charging along toward similar vague goals—sort of competing, sort of challenging; agreeing on ends and seldom on means—loving, but not always liking.

The year we met, I had gone to the Southwest Pacific with my P-38 squadron on the great troop ship Monterey. We sailed with the tide under the Golden Gate bridge and out across the Pacific, zigzagging at top speed to evade the enemy subs. Along with my fighter-reconnaissance squadron, a Red Cross unit shared the ship.

One of the loveliest girls I had ever met I found in a khaki Red Cross uniform standing beside the rail our first night out to sea. We talked for a while. Then some wild, mustached Aussies came and took her away. I was on watch so I had to stay on deck.

The next night the seas were rough and the decks were wet in rain. No one wanted to go to his bunk for fear of seasickness, so we gathered in a jammed passageway below decks. My heart leapt as I found myself sitting on the floor against the bulkhead squeezed in next to this lovely girl with the light brown hair. But to my utter dismay I soon found the Aussies had settled down opposite—and they were full of fun and interesting songs and games just made for this sort of sit-in. They were laughing and singing and she was laughing and singing, and I was miserable.

I wanted to talk to her alone. I wanted to touch her hair—to put my arm around her. The place was jammed and dimly lit and choking with cigarette smoke, so I asked her if she would like to get some air.

She nodded.

I jumped up and reached for her hand as the intercom crackled. We paused, and a voice said, "Now hear this. Lieutenant Bottomly, report to the Officer of the Deck immediately."

I glanced at my wrist. It was two minutes past eight—I was late for watch duty.

As the days wore by, the exciting adventure of going to war took on a new dimension of excitement. Her name was Betty. She called me "Bo" because she couldn't remember my real name. We sat together on the fantail and watched the evening movies. We climbed up onto the bow to watch flying fish leap ahead of the great prow. We leaned against each other in our ponchos when the drenching rain blackened the tropic night.

Hidden from the deck crowd by the pom-pom guns, we whispered and laughed softly and tried to hold back the moving hours. The Aussies began to disappear, and we began to hate the time after taps when the girls went up to the tennis deck to sleep while the men filed below or stood by the rail to smoke a last cigarette and stare at the new moon's bashful, black and silver dance upon the water. My heart had never before felt this warm and tender glow.

Then we came one dawn into Noumea harbor in New Caledonia. This was Betty's destination. This was the morning we had come to dread.

The ship was alive with excitement! Boats were being lowered. Names were being called out. Rosters were being checked. People were yelling good-byes. We stood together—her head under my chin, hair blowing about my face, tears but no sound.

Clinging.

Then she was gone.

I walked to the seaside of the deck. I couldn't watch that boat go away. Minutes passed. My heart had never been so brimming full. I knew I would never again see that tousle of light brown hair, that dazzling smile, those misty blue eyes.

Then from far out on the water of the bay, I heard her voice—through cupped hands—call out "Bo" with a little rise and fall. I rushed across the deck, between the scuppers, fell over the hose and crawled to the rail. Way out on the flat water a loaded whaleboat knifed toward shore. And standing there, a tiny khaki willow, brown hair blowing, waved and called my name.

The months flew by—on to Australia, on to Hollandia, on to the Halmahera Islands. Every day somewhere, under some sweating tent, I would pause from fighting and flying to scratch out a V-mail letter, mail it down the islands and hope and wait.

One day I joined a flight returning some of our airplanes down the chain of islands to a depot. We were to trade our war wearies for a newer model P-38. We landed, tired and wet in our ragged flying suits, and stumbled across the sun-baked ramp to the Red Cross Canteen. We were directed to hurry back, but we needed the lift of a cup of coffee and a doughnut before we headed north again.

The place was crowded with half-naked brown bodies in faded fatigue hats. We got in line and moved along to where the paper cups of steaming black were being thrust across from behind the counter. Chatting and laughing and shoving, I grabbed a cup and turned to go.

The voice was soft as velvet, yet it tinkled like a bell. "Hello, Bo."

I looked across the counter into a blue-eyed, sunburned smile that stopped my heart in midbeat. The brown hair, bleached by the sun, tumbled from under a funny khaki hat. I dropped my cup and it spilled all over the counter.

"Wha-wha-what are you doing here?" I stammered.

"I came up looking for you."

"I thought you'd forgotten. You said you'd write."

"I write every day."

The guys were shoving. "Come on, Bottomly! You're a fighter, not a lover. Keep it moving." Betty passed me another cup and touched my hand, and I was pushed out into the tropic noon. My guys grabbed me by each arm as I turned back. I saw her face, still watching me. She made a kiss with her mouth and the nipa door swung shut.

We flew and fought and the months raced by. We packed to move on to Clark Field in the Philippines. I went back once to the island depot, but Betty was gone.

Then one evening I flew a message packet back to Hollandia, our big base at MacArthur's Headquarters on New Guinea. I chocked my fighter, commandeered a jeep and roared up the mountain trail in a cloud of dust. I had to be back for a dusk take-off as the field was blacked out after dark.

At the guard gate on the hill I slid to a stop and fumbled in my flight suit pocket for my pass. The guard was busily chatting with the driver of another jeep leaving the compound. As I came up with my plastic badge, he moved to check me out.

The other jeep edged forward into gear and then someone yelled, "Stop!" I caught my breath. Leaning out of the back seat, brown hair flying in the wind, blue eyes large in surprise, sat the most wonderful shock of my life.

"Bo!" she screamed. "I've been looking all over for you!"

I delivered my pouch, but dusk drew down too fast, and I was forced to cancel my return flight plan and remain overnight. We stayed up all night talking and laughing. The next morning we climbed to the waterfalls behind the Red Cross compound and under the jungle canopy, happier than two people have ever been in the middle of a war, I asked Betty to marry me.

I saw her only one more time in the Halmahera Islands at a beach party somewhere. I think it was Biak. The next month she leapfrogged ahead of me to Leyte in the Philippines where she set up a lovely, nipa club on the beach for American GIs.

As the war moved on, my squadron jumped to Clark Field where on the third of July Betty and I were married in a little bombed-out church in Manila. The whole squadron was there. We held in our hands a letter of permission from the Commander-in-Chief, General of the Army Douglas Mac-Arthur—the only such permission he granted before the surrender. We both hoped someday to meet him and thank him.

1
up,
over
and out

It was broad daylight now. We reached our cruising altitude and raced east toward the pass. It was going to be an easy mission—a decisive mission—packed with glory. I spread out the formation again to watch for navigation points and enemy MIG fighters. My mind returned to its sweep through my life. What a beautiful, classic, driving charge up the military power structure it had been—so far!

As World War II drew to an end, we moved our P-38 squadron to Okinawa and then into Japan. We were based at Fuchu, an airstrip west of Tokyo. I was promoted to first lieutenant and raised to a more responsible job in the Fighter

Group Headquarters. This, in the back of my mind, validated again my wisdom in adhering to my power-oriented, existential philosophy.

One hot, muggy, late October day the Wing Commander, Colonel Joe Davis, called me back into his office. He was a short, stocky, handsome colonel—right out of *Twelve O'Clock High.* As I entered and saluted, Colonel Davis was tipped back in his chair—feet on his desk, hat cocked back on his head—swatting flies.

"At ease, Bottomly," he smiled. "Look, the war's over. One of these days all of us old duffers will be going home. I'm trying to decide which one of you young studs I should leave in charge. The wing has got a lot of responsibility—staying combat ready—photographing and mapping all of Japan and Korea. I don't want to leave some wild, drunken fighter jock in command.

"I want a good, solid leader—but a helluva flier that can set a good example in the air and on the ground. I've flown with most of you. I've watched you all work and play. But tell me, Bottomly, who do *you* recommend? Who is the best, most reliable, resourceful, all-around fighter pilot in the wing?"

"I am, sir," I responded without hesitation.

The fly swatter stopped in mid-swing. Colonel Davis' eyes narrowed.

His lips formed a very "blue" word, but no sound. His eyes swept carefully over me from head to foot and back as if he had never really seen me before. Then aloud, "That's what they told me."

"You mean your staff agrees I'm your best man?"

He shook his head. "Nope—but they all agreed you'd say you were. And I bet five bucks in the blind you wouldn't dare."

The colonel's hunch about rotation was right. December

came, and all the experienced old warriors went home— colonels, majors, captains—and he left me in charge. My first command. I was a twenty-four-year-old First Looey with a squadron of P-38s, a Japanese university for a headquarters, a Japanese fighter base and the village of Fuchu to supervise.

Joy and terror alternated as we pressed forward into the coldest winter Japan had faced for many years, and the villagers had almost nothing to live on or in. We shared what we had with them. In fact, I had shot the padlock off a warehouse full of impounded Japanese flight gear—flying suits, fur-lined jackets and boots—and issued them to the villagers.

The word got around and one day we had a visitor from Supreme Headquarters in Tokyo. He had been making a swing through our area, and he stopped by unannounced for dinner. He was thinner than I had expected and more bald. Although he had been in the villages, fields and factories all day, he had a clean, tailored, pressed look that made me feel—even in my freshest uniform—rumpled and frayed.

At dinner, he asked me about my village and about the curious phenomenon he had observed—old women and school children wearing military flying gear. I explained that we had several times sought guidance from headquarters on issuing the impounded supplies as a humanitarian measure. Yet the bitter winter wore on, and no guidance had been forthcoming.

I said that when the temperature went below freezing for a week without respite, and I began to lose village lives while the woolen clothing lay unused, I felt that common decency forced me to act under the traditional prerogatives of a field commander. So I used my best judgment and issued the clothing.

The general looked me in the eye for a long moment. Then he stood up and put his hand on my shoulder. "Lieutenant, I think you acted wisely. At least, you acted."

He smiled and turned away. As he did so, I signaled my adjutant to have his car brought up in front. But instead of leaving, he walked into our great dayroom next to the mess where he lit his pipe and began pacing back and forth before the fireplace, sipping coffee from a squadron mug. The general shook hands with each young fighter pilot and chatted a moment with him, looking him squarely in the eyes.

Most of my guys were telling our visitor that they were in the service for the duration and now were eager to get home and get out. He paused by the fireside and held up his cup.

"Gentlemen," he called out, "let me give you some advice. Don't be in such a hurry to get out of uniform. Next to serving God I have found serving country is the noblest pursuit of man."

He looked from one young face to another and spoke deliberately as though he were dictating an important letter.

"Whether you serve for a moment—as in casting your vote, or for a lifetime—as I have in the Army, this serving one's fellow man is essentially what separates us from the beast.

"Because we are so poorly paid, meanly treated and quickly forgotten, the profession of arms must be the most unselfish in the world. Yet in what other role can a man spend his life with his heart so filled with satisfaction—securing his country in order that happiness might be pursued by neighbors he doesn't even know. In what other profession could an ordinary lad like me have been able to so serve my countrymen, and yet thrill to the challenge of the call to the most exciting tasks man can be assigned—to explore, to teach, to minister, to fight, to doctor, to spy, to judge, to lead, to conquer—even to rule—in the name of God and the United States of America."

From somewhere appeared the general's legendary tan cap

embossed with old gold braid. A brown cape was thrown over his shoulders as he strode for the front entrance. His hand was a warm vise on mine.

Then the black Packard door slammed shut, as tires and gravel said goodnight. This was my first and last encounter with General of the Army, Douglas MacArthur.*

From being the first jet squadron commander in the Pacific, I returned home just in time to join in another first. The world was caught in the growing tensions of the Cold War. And now, in the fall of 1947, Berlin was under blockade.

The Communists had closed the land corridors from western Europe to the old capital. As another devastating winter approached, an airlift of food and fuel was set up to supply the beleaguered city. Then the Soviets began harassing these transports along the air corridors.

A young visionary lieutenant colonel named Dave Schilling, my fighter commander at Selfridge Field, Michigan, began planning how a squadron of jets could be flown to Europe to take the pressure off the air transport stream. Our entire planning team knew we could never hope to fly our little fighters directly across the Atlantic Ocean. But among our members were fliers who had fought in Europe during World War II, and they knew of a route by which short range fighter aircraft might be able to make it to the continent.

Circling over the Arctic lay an arc of island bases used during the war to ferry fighters and bombers to England.

---

*My 15 December 1945 diary entry concludes: "There goes one of the great generals of all time. I wonder if he ever was a lieutenant."

Years later, I was on a trip to Kabul, Afghanistan with Major General Arthur Trudeau, G-2 of the U.S. Army. I was thumbing through an old guest book in the great stone Regimental Mess of the famous Bengal Lancers when suddenly my attention was arrested by a flourishing signature: *Arthur MacArthur & Son.* And just below it scribed neatly in heavy black ink—*Douglas MacArthur, 2nd Lt. U.S. Army.*

Though some of the generals in the Pentagon were skeptical of our ideas, we charged ahead.

First, we measured the distances. Then we laid out these same distances on a map of the U.S. We found the same distances would be encountered if we flew from Selfridge to Jacksonville, Florida to Shreveport, Louisiana to Albuquerque, New Mexico to March Field, California to Wichita, Kansas and back to Selfridge. Through the spring and summer of 1948, we practiced this circuit again and again. Not one mishap occurred.

On the fifteenth of July, 1948, we launched 16 P-80 Shooting Stars from Selfridge Field to Bangor, Maine to Goosebay, Labrador to BW-1, Greenland to Keflavik, Iceland to Stornoway, Scotland to Odiham, England to Furstenfeldbruck near Munich in Germany. The first jet flight to Europe. What a thrilling experience for a young captain.

I remember standing up in the cockpit of my jet when we landed in the crowd at Munich and looking up at the snow-capped Dolomite Alps to our south, I shook my fist and shouted, "See, even some four-star generals can't appreciate that what man can conceive, man can achieve—if he has guts enough to try."

As a young lieutenant colonel, I worked my way into the position of Director of Operations of one of the great fighter-bomber wings in Europe. We were one of the first to place 48 sleek new jets—loaded with hydrogen bombs—on a twenty-four-hour alert. We were a vital part of the great tactical deterrent of the late '50s.

Each one of my pilots stood by, ready in his bunker with half the code to launch in his flying suit pocket. The other half I held ready to send him if the *alert* were sounded. What a tremendous responsibility for a young lieutenant colonel!

As the sands of the hourglass trickle down, so destiny was

flowing toward an appointed hour. I was hungry to make a large reach for power. The time to make this reach approached during the fall and winter of 1959.

I could see great weaknesses in our real combat readiness in Europe. I pointed these out repeatedly to my superior, a complacent, elderly colonel who had plateaued out in the service and who desired only to see his tour of duty completed in peace. He constantly admonished me not to make waves.

I pointed out to the colonel the need for at least a few crews to toss real atomic weapons at targets in the North African desert or in the ocean—even old, low-yield weapons, if necessary—to find out if our toss bombing methods would really work. We also needed to know if the flash shields in our F-101s would perform as advertised. We discussed the sad vulnerability of our above-ground combat command post. I suggested that loading crews should practice with real hydrogen bombs instead of dummies so that we could eliminate the "nervous" factor in a real emergency. I pointed out that heavy snows would ground us in winter because of inadequate snow removal plans and equipment.

On New Year's eve, 1959, I happened to be scheduled for the twenty-four-hour Command Post watch. As the evening wore on, I sortied out of the CP to visit the squadrons and the Officers' Mess. Parties were clustering everywhere on the base as pilots and wives and sweethearts enjoyed a warm celebration.

Sometime around 9:30 P.M., as forecast, it began to snow. By eleven o'clock, a deep, soft snow covered the parking ramps, the fighting aircraft, the taxiways and the runway. Inside the Officers' Mess, the NCO Club and the Squadron Party Rooms, joy and revelry prevailed.

I made one more reconnaissance around the airdrome at half past eleven. As the clock ticked toward midnight, any casual observer could see that—from the Wing Commander down to the lowest airplane mechanic—most everyone was enjoying a last hour of holiday. There was only a handful of sober fighter pilots, except for the alert crews which I knew were ready—ready except for the immobilizing snow.

Perfect!

Now was the time to punch the button and call a practice alert. This meant that when the siren blasted, the alert force would man their aircraft and taxi. When they reached take-off position, they would simulate a take-off and then return to their alert pads. All other fighter pilots would race to the flight line, brief quickly, load dummy weapons and take off for their practice alert targets far away over on the continent.

This main force monitored Command Post radio frequency awaiting the "Go," "No go" code word which was normally broadcast before the flights had reached the Belgian coast. If the "No go" was sent, all returned to base. If the "Go" was sent, all proceeded on to the assigned target and made a practice bomb run. This exercise was then followed by a critique where the miscues were explored and corrections ordered.

I walked into the Command Post at one minute before midnight. I took out the alert checklist and began the procedure. I threw the switch which sounded the great sirens mounted on and in buildings all over the base.

I spoke into the speaker system that connected the CP with every building on the airdrome. "This is a red alert. Repeat, this is a red alert. Report to your battle stations immediately. Carry out Exercise War Plan Alpha. Further instructions will follow."

I then called our higher headquarters, Third Air Force, and informed the duty officer in their Command Post that we were conducting a routine practice alert. I walked to the heavy door where a guard stood in winter gear securing entry to the CP. I threw it open. Outside, a swirl of snow swept the security lights with a white blur. The ground was blanketed in snow a foot deep.

I thought to myself: "The Wing Commander may find this a rude joke, but the four-star general at headquarters in Germany will say, 'What an unusual gutsy decision! Who called that alert? He should be promoted. We need more bold, tough commanders in this Air Force.'"

While phones rang in a mad crescendo behind me on the elevated console and colored lights flashed everywhere, out in the swirling darkness an amazing kaleidoscope of lights and sounds erupted. Car engines raced. People ran. Tires skidded in the slush. Women screamed. Fenders crunched. People shouted.

Chaos, it says, was the utter confused state of primordial matter before the creation of orderly form in the universe. That was RAF Station Bentwaters, England, as midnight tolled in 1960. And through the chaos, the incessant base siren from the tops of buildings howled relentlessly: "War! War! War! This is it!"

The carpet on the Commanding General's office was dark red. It was 1:00 P.M. on New Year's Day at Third Air Force Headquarters near London. I had been driven, splashing slush across the Midlands, and did not have to wait.

The general spoke slowly and without emotion. "Colonel Bottomly, you initiated the practice alert last night?"

"Yes, sir."

"Colonel Bottomly, you are an aggressive and imaginative young officer. I'm sure a great future is in store for you.

Unfortunately, we don't need men of your unique qualities in Third Air Force at this time. On the other hand, the War College is crying out for bold, perceptive, innovative men. I'm sending you there.

"I believe there is an airplane out of Mildenhall tomorrow. May I give you a direct order? Be on it!"

Naturally, I was surprised at this unexpected attitude. However, my dynamic philosophy taught that character is built on adversity, and a genius is one who has learned to turn a tactical disappointment into a strategic victory. I was determined to do this.

My year at the War College proved to be a happy, successful endeavor. I regained my confidence, and I strengthened my determination.

Then about this time, a very significant thing happened that eventually was to affect my total life pattern.

1
the
critical
years

My eldest son, Roc, whom I had raised in the same disciplined self-reliant mold in which I had been raised, decided to follow in his father's footsteps and serve his country. He elected to go to the Air Force Academy. When the choice youth of our country gather annually in July at Colorado Springs to start their great adventure there, they don't know each other. So, in an effort to match unknowns fairly, roommates are selected at random.

Roc chose or was chosen by and began to room with a young Navigator—not an airplane navigator, but a young Christian Navigator, named Ed Powell. This young man had a book that my son was not familiar with. This book addressed some basic questions that my son had not mulled over before: Who am I? Why am I here? Where do I go after I leave here? From the very beginning, late into the night—after "taps," by flashlight the two roommates shared from this unusual book, discussing its exciting concepts on the meaning of life.

One day I received a beautiful joy-filled letter from my son. He had become a Christian. Well, I was disappointed. I had taught him all I thought a young man needed to know about life. I had given him the four principles that my dad had taught me. I had fed him on Russell, Nietzsche and Fromm—plus a few concepts of life which I had developed myself, and frankly I wasn't very pleased that he had met a young stranger with a book and suddenly had chucked all my hard, real, human philosophy in the trash can to follow a mild medieval mystic who advocated free love.

Yet Roc was my eldest son. And I loved him with all my heart. We had hunted and fished together, played Little League baseball side by side, tramped the hills and fields of life hand in hand. So I dispatched a response from a warm heart. I told him that he was out in the great world now, and we had agreed that he would make his own decisions out there.

But I also reminded my son that he had been warned he would run into all sorts of creeps and kooks with weirdo philosophies. And sure enough, he had found one. Still, I counseled that it was probably a good thing. If he kept it in proper focus and didn't take it too seriously, religion might help him get a broader view of life.

At the same time, I admonished him not to take his eye off the ball—the real power of the universe. That power didn't lie out in some distant mystic heaven. It lay right directly under a man's navel. It was called *human will*. How each of us fueled that burning ember and exploited that power determined the mark he would leave upon mankind. I told him a strong, aggressive, virile man didn't need any crutches or crosses or Christs.

Well, being an intelligent, deliberate lad, my son had not wandered into his new relationship superficially or emotionally. He knew exactly what he had found—the key to life, and he encouraged me to get hold of this book and read it.

Every night Roc prayed that somehow, somewhere, sometime his old dad would find the time and the cause to pause a moment in life's racing career to listen to or read about the claims and promises that his young Navigator friend had shared with him. But I didn't have the time nor the inclination for any form of philosophic meditation in those days. I was a salmon plunging against the rapids of challenge, competition, adversity—the American scene.

It goes on every day of our lives in every city from coast to coast—in business, in commerce, in education, in the professions, in organized crime and in religion. My specific scramble was the military rank structure.

These years were critical in my assault on the battlements of power and success. This was my Gettysburg charge up the stairway to the stars—a phrase more real than figurative for a military man. Like most hungry, ambitious professionals, I had illusions of stars on my shoulders. I dreamt of being a general.

I've shared quiet thoughts with many of my contemporaries during the lull of battle or in the boredom of a long Pentagon war-room watch. The power syndrome begins rather innocuously: "If only I could make general—just one star—my ambitions would be fulfilled. My climb would be over. I would be satisfied and hand the reins of might over to the young."

Yet I have seen these selfless tigers reach that brigadier

general level. For a month or so all is warm and golden. The appetite for the fight seems to have been satisfied.

Then suddenly one morning this new glory isn't glory any more. The glitter has gone. The smiles and salutes and shouts have died. The pink-gold of success has turned to grey ashes in his mouth, and one quiet evening, he gazes up again—and sees another star.

During these critical, climbing, middle years, I used to have a vivid recurring dream. A shaft of sunlight sliced through a giant elm and bathed a patch of green behind the White House. I stood there straight as a ramrod before the President of the United States. He bent over pinning a new rank on my shoulder. Out of the corner of my eye, I glanced over. I was the first six-star general of the Armed Forces.

How much success will satisfy a man's ambition once and for all?

As General Brown had so succinctly put it, "Always just a little more."

On my fortieth birthday, I was promoted to full colonel and pushed up to the Joint Chiefs of Staff as Assistant Secretary. This was a very responsible assignment. I took turns with the Secretary, a remarkable brigadier general named Ingalito, taking the official notes of the meetings of the Joint Chiefs.

It was a real thrill to hear the door close on the "Gold Room" and sit with the four-star generals and admirals and listen to them discuss the mighty issues of state. It was my job to make a record of their conversations in shorthand. Then following each meeting we took these notes and drafted a "decision paper." This paper was the official government record of what the Chiefs of Staff had agreed to in that meeting.

One rather routine day in 1965, I was sitting in my office on the second floor of the Pentagon transcribing some meeting notes. There was a shadow in my doorway, and I looked up to find the Chairman of the Joint Chiefs of Staff. I popped to attention. I had never before been visited by the most senior officer of the Armed Forces—nor, to my knowledge, had anyone else in the building.

"Bottomly, quickly, bring your pad and follow me."

As we hustled down the hall and up the stairs, he briefed me that the Secretary of Defense had called an emergency meeting of the Joint Chiefs in the Secretary's office. There was trouble in the Tonkin Gulf. We swung to the right at the top of the majestic stairs and walked straight into the Secretary's conference room. Through the open door to the inner office I could see Secretary Robert McNamara talking on the telephone at his massive desk.

I sat at one end of the long conference table, opened my shorthand pad and date-timed a fresh page. In a moment an avalanche of humanity tumbled into the room. The four-star generals pushed past each other chattering excitedly. Several civilian defense officials and other government figures sat down in the chairs that lined the walls. As the Secretary came in he brought with him Dean Rusk, then Secretary of State.

My boss, General David Burchinal, Director of the Joint Staff, leaned over and whispered, "Bottomly, this may be the most important meeting of this decade. Get every word you can."

In a few moments over the speaker system from the National Military Command Post came a calm but intense voice describing a military action. The rise and fall in volume and the slight distortions in reception told me at once that we were listening to a radio broadcast. I began writing. Admiral David L. McDonald, Chief of Naval Operations, leaned forward and in a loud whisper informed those sitting at the table that we were listening to the captain of the U.S. destroyer

Turner Joy broadcasting direct—in real time over single side band radio—from the Gulf of Tonkin.

The captain, like a veteran sportscaster, described the action taking place on the dark waters of the gulf as his destroyer was attacked by communist torpedo boats. He described the play of the searchlights, the wake of passing torpedoes, the blast of gunfire. He did a superb job. The instinctive hunch that history was in the air arrested every fiber of every man in the room. Huddled around that long table, ears straining, were some of the most important men in government, listening intently as the radio transmission crackled and distorted, surging and fading, then booming out loud and clear only to fade again.

Soon the action was over. The conversation died and the destroyer's radio went off the air. For half an hour the chiefs and the secretaries exchanged views and proposals. A decision was made, and the meeting suddenly broke up.

Then just as I noted the time of adjournment on my steno pad, I felt a hand on my shoulder. Turning, I found myself looking up into the face of Washington's most famous bulldog.

"Son, when you get those notes transcribed, send a copy directly to me at the FBI."

"Sir, there's no way I can do that. These are the discreet discussions of the Joint Chiefs of Staff. The notes do not leave this building."

The muscles of his square jaw tightened, and his black eyes burned. There was a long moment of breathless impasse, then he turned away toward General Burchinal. I grabbed my steno pad with its historic notes, slid between the milling elbows and left the room.

Once in the hall I popped my pad under my arm and thrust my hands into my trouser pockets. I turned the corner of the giant staircase where I could look out the tall windows and across the Potomac. The dome of the Capitol glistened in the sunlight; its tiny flags flying.

I took a deep breath, exhaled and spoke out loud to myself. "Bottomly, if you can tell J. Edgar Hoover where to go and get away with it, you're too big for this job."

The Communist attacks on the U.S. destroyer *Turner Joy* that day, together with the decisions reached at that historic meeting, opened up the longest, the most costly and—apparently—the least decisive war in our history.

As the tempo of the action mounted, it was clear to me that the great adventures, as well as the bulk of promotions, were—as usual—unfolding in the combat zone. I volunteered, and after a year teaching young pilots to fight in the F-105 and later in the A-37, I arrived in Saigon as commander of a task force called Combat Dragon.

In the manner of Mad Anthony Wayne's Revolutionary War recruiting posters, I had recruited my band of freedom fighters from all over the Air Force with the following bulletin:

NOTICE

Men, what I have to offer you is sweat, fatigue, danger, disease and perhaps death; the chill of wet, cold nights in the open air; the depressing heat of the tropic sun, poor lodgings, combat rations, short munitions, long hours of hard fighting, dangerous guard posts, and the continual struggle to fly and fight and destroy the enemy. You who love freedom and like it tough, follow me.   Dragon 1

7

fly far,
dragonfly

For the better part of a year, we hunted the enemy in the Mekong Delta and around Saigon. We bombed, strafed and rocketed his bunkers, his camps and supply areas. We pounded his jungle canopy, his caves and tunnels, his river hideouts.

During this period we were testing the combat capability of a new airplane, the A-37. This plane was an inexpensive modification of our old, reliable Cessna primary trainer. Our task was to see how well this souped-up Sopwith Camel could perform various combat tasks and how well it could survive enemy ground fire. To our surprise, we found that this tiny jet was remarkably effective in most ground attack roles.

The A-37, nicknamed "The Dragonfly," could operate off modest runways. It was very versatile, easy to maintain, accurate at bombing and strafing, and—most amazing of all—it could carry the normal bomb load of a WWII Flying Fortress.

We tested the aircraft in all the major attack and support

roles normally called for in a limited war except aerial combat. Because of its subsonic speed, the A-37 was not at all suitable in combat against modern jet fighters. But overall, it proved to be very strong for its size and capable of producing fantastic sortie rates.

During November 1967 we were operating out of Pleiku in the central highlands testing the airplane in the interdiction role. Near the end of the month we got a surprise visit from Air Force Chief of Staff, General John P. McConnell, escorted by the theater air commander, General William W. Momyer. Both generals asked the pilots many questions about our ability to find and destroy enemy trucks hiding under the jungle canopy, to hit small moving targets like bulldozers at work on the roads and to escape enemy fire. And both men seemed pleased with our answers and particularly pleased with the enthusiasm of the ground crews.

As they completed their examination of our mini-armada of tiny fighters loaded with rockets and bombs and bristling with machine guns, they turned back to their T-39 jet to continue on to other war bases. General McConnell suddenly turned to me and asked, "Bottomly, how far will the airplane fly?"

I responded, "About a two hundred-and-fifty-nautical-mile radius is the longest combat mission we have flown."

"No, no," he countered quickly, "I mean how far could you ferry the airplane on a one-way flight?"

I just flat didn't know the answer to that one. In the six months our Combat Dragon task force had been evaluating the fighting capability of the A-37, we had been authorized by General Momyer to try every type of attack mission. We had flown the airplane against every type of combat target available in all four corps areas of South Vietnam. We had operated from very long and very short runways.

We had bombed bunkers with wall-to-wall 750 pounders; we had strafed enemy troops with nine miniguns firing forward; we had rocketed and we had showered CBU bomblets on supplies stacked in the jungle. We had even spent a couple of weeks as Forward Air Controllers (FACs)—calling in F-105 and Navy A-7 strikes on truck parks in Laos. We had flown armed reconnaissance and—most terrifying of all—night interdiction under flares.

Nonetheless General McConnell had caught us. I looked him straight in the eye and said, "Sir, I don't have the answer to that one, but I'll sure find out."

He put his hand on my shoulder and smiled, "I'll bet you will, Colonel."

The T-39's door swung up and, with "Spike" Momyer at the controls, it kicked a blast of highland sand in my face and was gone.

When a colonel gets caught without an answer to a four-star general's question, he doesn't let much grass grow under his feet. The next two days were drizzle, but the first day of December dawned clear and cool. We loaded an A-37, tail number 520, with full internal fuel and hung four 100-gallon pylon tanks on the inner bomb stations. This brought the takeoff weight of the Dragon Fly to 12,000 pounds—half airplane, half fuel.

The evening before I had flight-planned a very long course north and west over South Vietnam, Laos and Thailand. The route provided several options to turn for home should fuel consumption prove unexpected or should some tank fail to feed completely. I had estimated from the tech order figures, we could probably manage in the neighborhood of 850 nautical miles. Thus as I started for the revetment area with my survival gear, helmet and chute, I carried in my hand two 1 to 1,000,000 scale maps covering a large portion of Southeast Asia.

My crew chief, Tech. Sgt. Normal Hall and his assistant, Sgt. Bob Weaver, had gotten wind that we were going to go for an Olympic gold medal in range, so they were buzzing around the blue and white camouflaged aircraft when I arrived. Together we checked it over carefully and snapped down the fuel caps.

I climbed in and strapped down. Then I called Pleiku ground control and asked for a time hack. It was 1239—just past noon. I explained my call sign as Dragon 13 and said I was preparing to make a maximum range test flight.

The tower assured me I would not be delayed at the end of the runway. At 1241, I pushed the go switch on No. 1 engine. Within a minute both J-85s were humming and eager.

Without delay we completed the required checks and headed out of the revetment for the runway. The tower cleared me on without breaking stride. The jet spools howled, and 6,000 pounds of Cessna-General Electric teamwork coupled with 6,000 pounds of jet fuel burst out of the starting blocks, raced east along the tarmac ribbon and leapt into the cool highland air. It was 1246.

All systems were *go* on climb check. The pylon tanks fed evenly. I headed for the tri-state corner where Laos, Cambodia and Vietnam meet. That point of geography is miles north and slightly west of Pleiku. Riding the tech order climb figures up through broken clouds in 10 minutes, the altimeter eased to a stop at 30 grand directly over a bald mountain on the border called "Glendora." It is one of the key visual check points in the area where FACs and fighters have rendezvoused for years.

I nursed the spools back to 800 pounds per hour each. We settled down to a normal, on-the-step cruise at 336 knots true air speed: and with a direct crosswind out of Da Nang, this was also our speed over the ground.

The A-37 is not pressurized, so we normally did not venture above 25,000 feet during day-in-day-out combat operations. Nevertheless, I had decided that a ferry flight such as General McConnell had visualized would provide sufficient grounds for exception. Thus I chose to fly the first leg of my journey at 30,000 feet, a compromise between the outstandingly low fuel consumption at 35,000 feet and reasonable comfort and safety at 25,000.

It was a perfect day for flying. To my left I could see the interdiction strikes going in on Route 110 south of Attopu. Huge clouds of dust rose as the bombs exploded in the dry gravel.

The headset crackle of a Misty FAC checking in with PANAMA Radar Control made me turn my head to look, realizing as I did so that he was invisible over 100 miles east above the coast and heading north across the border into North Vietnam and high adventure. Every mission was high adventure for the Misties—F-100 jet fighters converted into Forward Air Controllers. These brave volunteers raced over North Vietnam at low altitude, dodging and ducking, spotting targets in areas too hot for our normal slow flying FACs.

The low whistle of the two jet engines becomes a part of the pilot and after a time he hears them no more. We dashed out across the rugged mountains of southern Tiger Hound, leaped the Xe Kong River and fled down the foothills toward the Mekong. Saravane, crouching by the SeDone Canal, ignored our whispered passing. Tchepon has a fingerprint which all Steel Tiger pilots know: four rivers and a bombed-out bridge. Yesterday at dusk she had favored me with a volley of cannon fire, as I reconnoitered for trucks down the Saynon River Valley. Today she slid by, quiet and harmless, six miles below.

North of Tchepon, the red earth cuts of the "chokes" glared

up ugly against the heavy green jungle carpet. These chokes are bombed out sections of road along the cliffs bordering the Nam Ng River where we tried to choke off the flow of supplies headed south toward the battle zone in South Vietnam and Cambodia.

The lacy net of the Ho Chi Minh Trail swept on north toward the karst canyon of Ban Phanop. Routes 23 and 1202 formed a white and tan net of by-passes and by-passes to the by-passes. I watched Route 912 crawl east through Ban Karai Pass into North Vietnam.

Suddenly, from behind a patch of stratus far below and east, the scar of Ban Laboy Ford broke into the clear. Just a tiny pink scar now, it was to become in the next year one of the more famous interdiction targets of the war. This ford across the Xe Kong River was sometimes called "Keegan's Folly"—so named after the stubborn Seventh Air Force Intelligence Chief who was determined to keep it closed to enemy traffic. Thus he ordered it bombed daily through most of 1968 until a scar was torn in the jungle visible for 50 miles on a clear day.

The radio was almost silent now save for F-105 flights returning from "up north." About every 10 minutes one of them checked in to get set up with a flying fuel tanker. Knowing that each flight was just a few minutes out of hell. I was thrilled by the pilots' cool, professional voices and crisp, no nonsense procedures. I thought, "Fighter pilot, you've come a long way, baby!"

I have never been able to fly northwest across central Laos without glancing anxiously into the amazing karst, limestone canyons that form historic Ban Karai and Mu Ghia Passes. I know that if I'm very close when I glance, I'm apt to pick up some thirty-seven-millimeter slugs in a wing, because these passes are cuts through the mountain border separating friendly Laos and enemy North Vietnam. Today I gave the canyons a wide berth and hurdled the Mekong to relative safety in Thailand.

The radio voice of "INVERT Control" spoke the outbound heading from Nakhon Phanom to Vientiane and verified that they had me on their radarscope. We banked west a few degrees and watched redwood forests chase the blue water of the Nong Han under our left wing and out of sight. "IN-VERT" radar control center handed DRAGON 13 a frequency change and a new voice called "BRIGHAM" advised that we were to fly a heading of 290 degrees for 90 miles to arrive over the Laotian capital city.

We sped on through the high, still Asian midafternoon.

Vientiane is suddenly there, and I'm not ready for it. That's what often happens when a pilot turns downwind and allows his thoughts some slack rein. I had flight planned that I would be seeing "pylon tank empty" warning lights on this leg and would then make the clubhouse turn at Vientiane and dash south for Ubon, shutting down one engine to gain economy without losing too much airspeed at the reduced weight. But no fuel lights glowed.

I now took the one extra option I had open—one I had hoped for and carefully worked over in my flight planning. I headed straight north directly away from home toward the fabled Laotian summer capital of Luang Prabang, then on to Dien Bien Phu and Hanoi. Highway 13 wriggled up along the Nam Ngum River and then burst out across the storied Planes des Jarres. I felt as if I were flying into a Steve Canyon adventure in that ancient troubled land.

My craft was obviously getting lighter in weight. I could creep the throttles aft a little and still hold the same speed and altitude. Chiang Mai, the jewel city of North Siam, the opium smuggling hot springs, resort center and leper colony spread out on the pretty Ping River down to my left. Down in the bluing east, fabled Route 7 climbed its tortuous way up onto the plateau from whence it would plunge down across North Vietnam to the Tonkin Gulf.

A red light flashed on the warning panel and then blinked out. This experience to a pilot is always accompanied by a rush of ice water down his spine. I knew that light meant my pylon tanks were finally going dry. I'd been expecting it; nevertheless, the scarlet flash brought the inevitable shot of adrenalin.

I sat tall on my survival kit and stretched my neck to see far ahead. Out there a scattered flock of mountain sheep grazed at about 10,000 feet, and down through them I could see the great horseshoe of the Mekong River pointing its northern finger toward the bosom of Burma.

I thought, "I've got it made! With pylons empty at Luang Probang, I can cut down an engine, retrace my path to Vientiane, check in by radio at our base at Udorn and then scat out across the red flats of Thailand for Ubon. Once there, home base will be an easy one hundred-and-fifty-mile glide."

The pylon tank warning light flashed again! I waited. I wanted a steady *on* signal before I switched to my tip-tanks—to make sure I'd burned every drop. At 1415 hours the light blazed steadily. I snapped the tip tank fuel switches up and rolled my tiny craft into a shallow bank.

As I looked out across northern Laos, a strange chill swept up my spine—just across the border in North Vietnam, historic Dien Bien Phu nestled darkly in the Song Ma valley. It now showed no scars to remind one of its status as a timeless milestone on the road to colonialism's utter and final defeat. My scalp crawled at the thrill of being there—of looking straight down upon one of world history's most exciting turning spots.

How transitory fame. Today Dien Bien Phu didn't look

like much at all—just a little, tan, grass-roofed village on a river. Nonetheless, it brought me an involuntary visceral twitch. I felt the same breath-catch I had felt years before standing on the plains of Arbela in Iran, sitting on the beach at Marathon in Greece, leaning among the ruins of Carthage, riding the hills overlooking the Little Bighorn and circling low over Omaha Beach . . . and curiously none of these places had looked like much at all.

Then the moment passed and, looking north, I caught my first glimpse of Red China. Involuntary goose bumps rose on my back and the hair on my arms moved as my gaze crept across the mountains, the rivers and the endless plains of Yunan and Kwangsi. Then something inside me turned my eyes away, as though I were forbidden to look. And I found myself scanning the blue-black sky to left and right and behind. All safe—no contrails anywhere.

Far below to the east lay Hanoi and the great MIG fighter base on the Red River. The sight was at once terrifying and exhilarating. Now I was testing the radar detectability of my tiny plane. Not only did its sky blue and white camouflage make it difficult to pick up visually against a cloud-patched sky, but also its tiny silhouette flying so high and far away should make no trace on the watchful North Vietnam radar-scopes.

But I couldn't be sure, so the adrenalin was there and the knot in my gut made me review how I intended to cope tactically should a flight of MIG 21s jump out of the green and brown quilt below. My hunch was that an attacking supersonic fighter would not be able to spot me in the sky, and if he should, he would go by so fast he could not get off a well-aimed shot.

Now Burma swept into view as my wide lazy turn pushed our nose across its fourth nation in 30 seconds. I was as far into the mystic hinterland of Kipling's Orient as I should probably ever be again in my life.

The great China Highway snaked south toward the Mekong scarring the jungle below. I rolled over on my back and looked directly down to verify my farthest point of northerly penetration. Then I turned for home. The clock on the instrument panel read 1420 (2:20 P.M.). I jotted that on my knee pad and, as the compass crept up on 160 degrees, I leveled the wings.

The time had come when according to plan, I must shut down an engine to save fuel. Reaching for the throttle controls, I pulled the left one back to idle and lifted it over the stop. The RPM dropped quickly to zero. I eased the right throttle wide open, and with full rudder trim, I found I still had to hold a few pounds of right foot pressure. This was going to get tiresome, but I had to fly exactly in trim or lose efficiency.

The airspeed bled steadily off . . . 170 . . . 160 . . . 150 . . . 147. I tried to be careful not to drop below flying speed, yet I did. The little craft shuddered in a stall. I could not maintain that altitude on one engine; not at this weight and dragging those four empty pylon tanks. I made a note.

Now holding 147 knots—and holding my breath as well—I watched us sink gently down through the empty ether. I was letting my little bird find its own steady speed altitude. We stabilized at 27,400 feet and leveled off. Almost in silence now, we swept south across the river toward Udorn.

Thailand was a brown and red Persian carpet, patched with the smoke of slash-and-burn farming. A small, white blot of stratus covered the joint U.S.-Thai airbase at Udorn. The village nearby was a gray finger of dust beside the river.

I could picture the thousands of busy people shuffling through the market, paddling along the dike or laughing and chatting in the dusty street. Busy on his own errand, intent on his own business, each one would be wrapped in his own world, largely unconcerned with the endless war—yesterday already forgotten, today a consuming drama, tomorrow still out of sight, out of mind; each one worrying a little, hating a little, dreaming a little, loving a little—yet all just flotsam on the river.

The warning light panel flashed red again! Tip tanks empty. The clock read 1504 and the TACAN said we were 20 nautical miles northwest of Ubon—our great jet base near the Mekong River in eastern Thailand.

The airplane had lost weight burning fuel, and so holding a constant airspeed, it had begun to climb gradually. Over Ubon, I switched engines, bringing in the left and snuffing out the right. We had established this as standard procedure to keep engine time even and to keep within limits the oil spill which occurs during engine windmilling. I jotted a note on my knee pad—Ubon at 1508 hours—1830 pounds of fuel remaining.

My left wing dropped, and I changed course to due east, crossing the Mekong once again. Southern Laos was patched with scattered to broken stratus clouds far below. Down to the left rose the dramatic, high, green mesa, Le Plateau de Boullon, its cliff faces laced with waterfalls.

My radio crackled, "Dragon 13, this is LION."

"Go ahead, LION. Dragon 13 here."

"Dragon 13, recheck your radar transponder. We are not receiving your squawk."

"Everything is go—circuit breaker checked."

"I can get a skin paint on you periodically, Dragon 13, but no transponder. Your path is paralleling the Cambodian border. Are you in the clear?"

The LION radar center controller was concerned because

U.S. aircraft were not allowed to cross into Cambodia without special clearance.

"Roger, LION, I have visual reference to the Xe Kong River and can visually identify the border geography."

"Dragon 13, recommend you adjust your course 15 degrees left until you pass Attopu. My track on you shows you too close to the border. This constitutes a border warning. Acknowledge, Dragon 13."

"Roger, I'm turning left to 075 degrees and recycling my transponder."

Far to the east towering cumulus clouds pierced the troposphere above the Annamite Mountain chain—the mighty north-south spine of Vietnam. The same strong northeast monsoon winds which had piled up those thunderheads were crowding me closer and closer to the out-of-bounds markers along the Cambodian border. Anticipating another worried call from radar control, I hiked in an extra five-degree wind correction and checked my air speed.

I was a little slow. I was getting light on fuel and the aircraft had bobbed like a cork back up to 30,000 feet. At that altitude we were biting into a one hundred-and-thirty-knot quartering cross wind from the left. I spotted the village of Attopu creeping under my left wing. There the river breaks north along the mesa and then loops east into the high Annamites.

On the surface, six miles below, shadows were lengthening and evening was falling on the deep jungle. Now I pointed my little craft's nose once again at the tri-border tip where Cambodia and Laos meet the long western flank of South Vietnam. Beyond, the wide and fertile Dak To Valley rolls east to the China Sea.

Smoke puffs rose from half a dozen redoubts where Fourth U.S. Division cannoneers were pounding away at enemy bunkers. From my high perch, this was the only evidence that down there the jungle and the hillsides thundered with artillery fire. Major General William Peers and his Shamrock Division were locked in one of the most decisive and bloody battles of 1967, the Battle of Dak To.

As we approached the border, I changed radio frequencies and checked in with PEACOCK, the radar control agency for the central highlands. It was 1555 on the clock. I had been airborne three hours and ten minutes. Slowly . . . tortuously slowly, my tiny cork bobbed east past the tri-border point, and I was safe—clear of the Cambodian border.

My leg was now numb from holding right rudder. As I let the right wing dip and the nose slide south, I also checked the trim to reassure myself that I had full left trim to compensate for the offset thrust of flying on left engine only. The heading 155 degrees aimed us southeast for the USAF fighter base at Phu Cat.

A fuel check showed about one-half hour of JP-4 remaining. My plan at this point was to ride down the hypotenuse of the triangle toward Phu Cat near Qui Nhon on the east coast of South Vietnam. Then at the point of no return when my last "fuel low" warning light came on, I would turn directly southwest and let down to Pleiku, my home base.

I suddenly discovered I was so hungry, I could eat a water buffalo, mud and all.

Time 1610 . . . fuel 500 pounds . . . position seven miles directly above the tiny Army helicopter strip of An Khe. Over my right shoulder I could see Pleiku due west under scattered popcorn clouds. No sweat on weather. My flight plan called for a landing with 300 pounds or about 20 minutes of fuel reserve.

I leaned my head gently to the right and squeezed the left throttle back to idle. As if we were one thing, my tiny bird and I rolled gently over and headed down and away to the west. This was it—the last leg home. Nose almost level, power all the way back, the saucy Dragon Fly glided lightly, gently back to earth. With a fifteen hundred-feet-per-minute rate of descent, I found I could hold 150 knots and this would give me 20 minutes to reach the runway at Pleiku.

I asked PEACOCK control to clear me to tower frequency. "Pleiku Tower, Dragon 13, request landing instructions."

"Dragon 13, stand by." The voice was terse. "All aircraft hold clear of the Pleiku Control Zone and maintain radio silence. We have a combat emergency in progress."

Oh, no!! A quick chill rifled my innards. I squirmed uncomfortably on my aching buttocks. I dropped my left wing to spot Phu Cat directly behind me. It was covered with cloud and 50 miles upwind from me. That would be too far to try.

Fuel 450 pounds.

I began a turn to the east, then bent it back around to the west—indecision. The bony fingers of panic inched up my throat. I'm going to blow it all by running out of gas.

Who could be having a shot-up airplane? Probably someone not able to get his gear down—and just when I had nowhere else to go.

How come PEACOCK radar hadn't advised me? I quickly punched PEACOCK's radar control frequency back in and asked the nature of the emergency at Pleiku.

"How long is it expected to last?" I queried.

The voice I heard in my jet helmet put an extra twist in the knot forming in my stomach. For the voice was unintelligible—it was the pidgin English of a Vietnamese student controller who had just come on duty. I repeated my request. He repeated his best effort.

Fuel 400 pounds.

This was building up toward one of those classic situations

that Flying Safety Officers lecture on for years after—a high ranking officer, endeavoring to enhance his prestige by some kind of glory flight, establishes a new record. Then he has to bail out in the pattern or crashes on landing because of some stupid, low probability, unrelated, diabolical quirk of fate—such as a fuel truck unexplainably stalling at the center of the active runway, a herd of water buffalo stampeding on the airstrip or an earthquake splitting the runway down the center.

Fuel 350 pounds!

I switched to emergency radio channel and listened. There was nowhere I could now divert and have any fuel reserve at all. I had boxed myself in to Pleiku, and now the runway was closed for an emergency of unknown duration.

Well, this is it, stupid! I could visualize the headlines in *Stars & Stripes:* "Colonel Blows Test, Sets World Record, Then Bails Out in Traffic Pattern."

The youthful voice of a troubled Forward Air Controller broke the silence: "Pleiku, this is Covey 04. I'm five miles west. My left gear is shot off, and I'm coming straight in. Put the fire truck at the middle turn off and chase those A-37 crew chiefs off the grass by the runway."

"Roger, Covey 04."

I visually picked up the tiny gray spotter plane floating in toward the Western approach. I judged from his distance out he would touch down in roughly three minutes. That would leave the ground crew seven minutes to clean up the mess and open the airstrip. I notified the tower of my gathering problem and went back to standard tower frequency and floated in toward a down wind leg—holding as much altitude as I could at almost idle power.

Fuel 300 pounds!

I hoped the gauge was conservative. I had never felt an airplane so light and bobbly.

The FAC pilot gingerly, cautiously approached then gently touched his little Bird Dog down. He held up the left wing with aileron and rudder. I leaned with him in my cockpit.

Beautiful!

He crept slowly left, then the wing suddenly sagged and the wing tip scraped the runway. Dust and sparks flew. Almost immediately he spun into the grass beside the runway just short of the center turn-off. As if by magic a platoon of A-37 crew chiefs and emergency ground crews surrounded the tiny gray bird. I could not believe my eyes, as they picked it up bodily and walked away to the parallel taxiway and set it gently down.

I calmly called, "Dragon 13 on downwind," started my left engine, checked power and in two minutes touched down. My fuel gauge showed 100 pounds. I taxied to the end and heaved a giant sigh of relief. I paused to check out my aircraft.

Almost immediately I was surrounded by the same crowd of concerned crew chiefs and emergency men who had saved me a minute earlier by carrying my friend away. There were cheers, shouts, smiles and for a moment I thought I was going to be bodily picked up in my airplane and transported to the revetments as had the tiny spotter airplane before me.

These faithful ground crews had scanned the skies since midafternoon when normally an A-37 would run dry of fuel. I was hours overdue, so they were sure I was lost, having fallen from the sky for lack of fuel. Now that I had made it, they all sported proud and joyful faces. The wanderer had returned.

Finally, they let me taxi back to the revetment area. Dozens rode along, sitting on my wings and pylons, all joyously a part of the great adventure. I jotted down the time . . . 1635.

The Pleiku tower called in my touchdown time as 1631, and the computer engineers went into a huddle. The crew chiefs popped open a can of coke, and we sat—like a row of blackbirds—on the wing making out the official forms. I felt like my old friend Charles A. Lindbergh landing in Paris!

Once in a while in life one does something really exciting that doesn't hurt anyone else in the world!

I felt the utter warm glee of glory for about five minutes as I finished the paper work. Then a smelly flying suit edged up beside me. I recognized, standing in it, one of my favorite spotter pilots. He was the one-wheeled Covey FAC that had just landed ahead of me. A scrub scar marked his forehead, but he was not concerned about himself.

Grinning sheepishly, he said, "Colonel, I'm sorry I got shot up and almost loused up your homecoming. We were all sweating you out on the radio—then I got hit and had to make a dash for home. I knew I should have landed on the taxiway, but I lost my nerve."

I grabbed the guy in my arms and hugged him tight. These Forward Air Controllers were consistently the real giants of this war, and I held in my grip that day's real hero.

Nonetheless, my A-37 Dragon 13, on 1 December 1967 flew 1414 nautical miles while airborne 3 hours and 45 minutes. I landed with 15 minutes of reserve fuel.

This was a new world's record!

I could now answer General McConnell's question. In all, it had been a day of little significance in aviation history, but one of total beauty, pride and joy for me and my little band of Combat Dragon pilots and crew chiefs.

We opened a case of beer and sang some old war songs to the lowing of the water buffalo in the paddy behind operations.

8
hit my smoke!

For two years the Combat Dragons fought—strafing and bombing in the Mekong River delta and Third Corps Area around Saigon, then further north along the Ho Chi Minh Trail. At the same time, we supported forces in some of the bloody battles for the Central Highlands like Dak To, Kontum and the Ashau Valley.

One day I was discussing future operations with the officer in charge of the air war in Southeast Asia, General George S. Brown. This guy was by far the finest combat commander I have ever worked for. As I turned to leave his office, General Brown put his arm around my shoulder and escorted me to the door.

Addressing me by the nickname my wife had given me during our courtship days, he said, "Bo, you have been here almost two years now. You are eligible to go home whenever you choose. But all of your training and experience—all those taxpayers' dollars have been for one thing—to prepare guys like you and me to fly and fight for our country when we're called.

"There's a war going on here—an unpopular war—and most people don't want to be associated with it. But we're professionals. We ought to be where the action is.

"If you would consider volunteering for another year, I will give you command of my strongest fighter wing, and you'll have a good shot at promotion to brigadier general."

At last it had come—the opportunity I had been waiting for! I snapped it up and, before a month had passed, I was on my way home to complete my Task Force Study and to get refresher training in the F-105.

In July, 1969, I returned to Southeast Asia as commander of the great base and fighter wing at Takhli in Thailand. Way back near the Burma border in west-central Thailand, the Allied Command had bulldozed out a two-mile strip of jungle and bush and laid in one of the most potent packages of military fighting power that has ever been assembled in the history of man.

I had over a hundred fighting airplanes: four squadrons of F-105 fighter bombers to launch out across the Mekong River and smash the enemy's supplies and bridges and truck convoys, missile sights and military complexes; two squadrons of electronic reconnaissance aircraft to search the enemy radar patterns and confuse him about the size and location of our strike forces; and a squadron of great silver tankers to refuel our fighters in the air coming and going on the long missions over northern Laos and North Vietnam.

Every morning we would open the day's flying activities before dawn. Our booming afterburners cracked the tropic stillness as we roared out to find and to destroy the enemy.

As the year progressed I found myself riding one of the greatest waves of power and glory a tactical air commander could dream of. We were tops in bombing accuracy. We led the theater in sortie rates. Our losses were low. I was really riding a great crest of success.

At the time, President Lyndon B. Johnson was in the White House. And he was not riding any great crest of success. In fact, he was under heavy attack, under mounting pressure from all sides to wind down the war. World opinion, the American press, student groups—all were critical of our role in the conflict.

The Vietnam War was lasting longer than any war our nation had ever been in. It was costing more in money and material resources than any war we had ever fought. Yet we didn't seem to be getting anywhere.

After serious, extended conferring and soul searching, the President one day went on national television and announced to the world that he was declaring a "bombing halt." He said in effect that the American Air Force was going to stop bombing in North Vietnam. We were going to stay out of North Vietnam. Instead, we would send representatives to Paris to sit down with representatives of the other side and—like civilized humans—we would endeavor to reason our way to a fair and lasting peace.

When the order to cease bombing targets in North Vietnam came out to the war zone, the fighter pilots laid their navigation maps out on the flight planning tables. There, with a big, black felt pen, we drew heavy lines around the border of North Vietnam on our maps. This measure was to help prelude our inadvertently crossing the border. The President had given his word to the world that we could stay out, and commanders at all levels carefully admonished each aircrew: *no one must cross!*

We had launched on time, burst out above the monsoon drizzle into the star-filled halls of night, joined up and spaced out, refueled and were now headed in on course to the target—Mu Ghia Pass. Our mission for the day was to cut the enemy supply route through the pass. Mu Ghia Pass was a narrow defile through those mountains that lay along the border between North Vietnam and Laos. Through this pass snaked a road, one of the main supply routes for enemy war materials.

Up ahead now, I could see the cut in the mountains. I rocked my wings to pull the flight in closer and then set up to circle once—well west of the border. Just south of the pass I rolled into a turn and bent my course around to the north.

It was dawn, but the pass was obscure in purple shadows. My flight fell in trail behind me. I checked my watch. Five past six. Good. Right on time over target.

Suddenly the sun popped out of the South China Sea and sat on the eastern horizon. I watched it thread its long yellow fingers through the mountains and unlock the pass. The road, a yellow-white snake, crawled along the northern cliff.

I called on the radio, "Hang high."

So the flight circled the battle area at altitude while I prepared to put in a marker bomb. The wind was out of the north, and we had to bomb parallel to the border to keep from crossing over on our pull out, so I rolled in from the south and pointed the nose straight down. At 500 knots I put the sight pipper just above the road on the side of the cliff. When the altimeter flashed past 10,000 feet, I "pickled" off one bomb and pulled about 5-Gs around to the left and up.

I glanced over my shoulder as the long nose of my "thud" crossed the horizon. Boom! A white flash in the canyon and a plume of smoke arose. Then great chunks of granite and karst and rubble roared down the cliff, covered the road and plunged on into the canyon below.

It was a good hit, so I called over the radio, "Hit my smoke!"

This command signaled my flight to aim right for that spot. Above the climbing sun, I caught the flash of a sapphire against the morning sky as my wingman rolled and plunged into the canyon. Down, down, down he dropped like a falcon.

At this moment, from the North Vietnamese side of the border, came a withering barrage of red balls—37-mm. anti-aircraft fire! This was a clear violation of the "no bombing agreement": if we didn't bomb across the border, they wouldn't fire across the border.

Several of the rounds hit my wingman. He reported "on fire" and headed west for the river. I called the flight to continue the strike while I peeled off to pick up my wounded buddy and escort him to safety.

We fled down across the Mekong Valley trailing black smoke, hydraulic fluid and pieces of aluminum—looking frantically for an emergency landing strip. At last, there it was dead ahead—the long concrete runway at Ubon, just across the river in friendly territory. I called the tower and got clearance for a straight-in landing.

His touchdown was perfect. He popped his chute to decelerate. Then . . . whoom! His airplane was enveloped in a great scarlet ball of fire.

The rescue crew lifted him out of the wreckage, an ambulance appeared, and sirens screamed open a path for him to the Ubon hospital. Standing there beside him in the emergency room, I could see he was badly burned—deep, black, charred all over. I turned and stumbled out into the tropic morning in a daze of anger and hatred and shock and revenge. I wandered across the field toward the flight line—clenching and unclenching my fists, taking one deep breath after another—as I fought to regain control of myself.

As I came up beside my fighter, I heard a roar overhead. Looking up, I saw my strike force sweep by. They had completed their mission, reformed and were headed west for our home base at Takhli. The thought floated across the screen of my mind, "I must follow them home."

But I didn't!

Instead I climbed into my airplane, secured the straps, taxied into position and blasted off to the east.

Climbing high, I crossed the Mekong River.

I crossed Mu Ghia Pass at high altitude. Far below in the disputed area that demarked the North Vietnamese border, I spotted the antiaircraft site that had shot down my friend.

Then I rolled my F-105 over and aimed straight down at the enemy battery. In one mass salvo, I dropped my entire bomb load. A direct hit! A magnificent explosion shook the earth and sky.

It smashed all their guns, killed all their crews and burned all their supplies. A towering column of black smoke and fire rose slowly into the tropic air. I could still see it climbing as I crossed the Mekong and headed for home.

The strike in the pass was scheduled to terminate at six-thirty. At six thirty-five a light reconnaissance airplane moved into the pass to assess the success of our attack on the road. He was still circling over the mountains when a giant explosion to the east rocked his tiny plane. He was mystified, but he concluded that this was a violation of the "no bombing order," so in accordance with instructions, he called in a special report to his Command Post which was immediately forwarded to Headquarters.

I had just landed back at my home base at Takhli and shut down my engine when my Executive Officer burst across the street and met me as I climbed down the ladder. The general wanted to talk to me on the telephone.

"Bo, I see you were fragged to lead a strike in Mu Ghia Pass this morning."

"Yes, sir, we closed the pass."

"I have a report here that some of your bombs apparently fell across the border in violation of the President's no-bombing agreement. Or is the report a mistake?"

"It's no mistake, General. The enemy fired at us in violation of the agreement and have probably killed one of your finest pilots and one of my best friends. I retaliated."

My boss was a gentleman. Nevertheless, he fully and instantly appreciated the dimensions of this infraction of the Rules of Engagement. He immediately grasped the political implications—the international repercussions that would surely follow. But above all, he knew and I knew that this act represented a classic breach of basic flying and command discipline. The mission had not been flown as briefed.

In a calm, low key, he explained his disappointment in my violation of his trust. He explained that only one other pilot had attacked across the border since the President had given his word to the world that we would stay out of North Vietnam. A light spotter aircraft had flown across the demilitarized zone north of Hue and had fired some smoke rockets at a fishing boat. In order to make absolutely certain every pilot in the theater recognized that violations of air discipline would not be tolerated, that young lad had been court-martialed and was currently serving two years in the penitentiary at Fort Leavenworth.

The general terminated our conversation in a cool, quiet voice: "You're suspended from command, Colonel. But stay close to a telephone until I inform you where *your* court-martial will convene."

1
the taming of the dragon

Stunned and limp, I slumped down into a chair. The shock of seeing my young friend burned alive, the blood-chilling violence of my exploding counterattack and now this career-shattering blow all within the hour left me shaken to the marrow and drenched with sweat.

I couldn't assimilate what had just happened. It was too much at once. It was like slugging down a triple-Scotch and then trying to stand up and walk away, casual-like. It couldn't be done.

Slowly I wrenched my eyes open and found myself looking down at the telephone still in my hand. I fumbled it back onto its cradle.

Two hours ago I had been on top of the world—the greatest hero in Southeast Asia—marshaling my force to make the most decisive strike of the interdiction campaign—about to win the Air Force Cross. Suddenly I was at the bottom of an asphalt pit, clawing to survive—the walls of the pit falling in about me.

I shook my head to clear my vision. Then I got up very carefully. I picked up my hat and, aware of nothing but a heavy ringing in my ears, I walked out of my office. I stumbled across the street and headed for my hooch in the command compound—400 yards away.

I could feel myself drifting down into a dreadful depression of disappointment, disaster, doom. I could hardly get my breath as gloom and guilt, anxiety and apprehension held me in their grip.

For three days, I walked toward my hooch. I passed through shops, offices, barracks, warehouses, bomb dumps, flight lines—face blank as though in deep thought. Inside, my gut was twisted in a knot of overpowering dread, and before my eyes raced a montage of terror. I could see prison doors clanging shut behind me.

Through the ringing in my ears I could hear the voice of a court-martial judge echoing down a long hollow corridor, "Give him 20 years . . . 20 years . . . 20 years."

Finally, toward the end of the third day, as dusk cast her violet veil out of Burma across the river, I found my hooch. In the drawing shadows, I stumbled through the door and collapsed on the edge of my bunk. I sat there a moment and then my head fell forward into the palms of my hands. I was weak from hunger, sick to my stomach with despair and absolutely exhausted.

I don't know how long I rested there. I remember one time

with all my strength raising up my head and heaving a great, hopeless sigh. Then my head fell back into my hands.

After a little while, a strange thing began to happen. The kaleidoscope of images and sounds that had harried me for over 48 hours began to slow down, quiet down, fade and die away. As the moments passed I became aware that, there on the black velvet screen of my mind, was the quiet face of my Christian son. Roc's image was clear and strong, and it persisted . . . persisted . . . persisted.

Someone was trying to tell me something!

I knocked the telephone off its cradle and asked the operator to get hold of my son. He had already graduated from the Academy and was now at Purdue University. The operator relayed my message to the MARS station and in about 10 minutes my son's buoyant voice came over the wire. I explained to him that violent disaster had struck me. I had suddenly been demolished and had come to him for help.

As though he were not surprised, but rather had been waiting for me to call, he replied, "Dad, I can help you—as I've mentioned in many of my letters—when you're ready to turn your life over to the Lord and become a Christian."

"Whaddya' mean? I am a Christian. I've been an honest, upright, church-going Christian off and on all my life."

"Hold it, Dad. I don't mean that. Going to church and living an honest, upright life doesn't make you a Christian. You are hiding behind the term 'Christian,' so you won't be labelled a Muslim or a Hindu or a Buddhist or—what you really are—a pagan. No, you're not a Christian.

"Dad, to be a Christian, you've got to believe in Jesus Christ—to believe what He said, what He did, what He is."

"Well, I generally believe what He said."

"Come on, Dad, you don't even know what He said. And there's no way you can *generally* believe what Jesus Christ said. You either believe it, or you reject it. You obviously reject it."

"Wait a minute! How do you know I reject it?"

"A rational man like you, Dad, cannot believe and trust in the claims, the promises and the works of Jesus Christ and live his life the way you live. You have deliberately turned your back on God and have determined to go it alone in this life.

"Your priorities give you away—personal power, glory, wealth, status—those aren't Christ priorities, Dad. Those are man priorities—those are your personal priorities.

"You see, Dad, the life-style you have chosen is *you*-centered. The Christian life that I would like to share with you is built upon a love and faith in God. It's God-centered.

"You see, a Christian simply has discovered that fellowship with God is the most important thing in a man's life. Of his own free will, he has accepted Jesus Christ as his Saviour and Lord. He believes what He said and has chosen to walk with Him. Thus his life moves along an entirely different path according to God's plan rather than according to your plan.

"You can see the difference. Take my roommate, Peter, for example. He has been a Christian for almost five years and enjoys a beautiful, close walk with the Lord. You can see it in his attitudes, his actions, his reactions, his expressions, his simple open honesty, his concern for others, his patience, peace of mind, his readiness to serve, his ability to suffer without complaining, his buoyant, positive, optimistic enthusiasm.

"All day long, his attitudes and activities reflect his faith and trust in God. Let's face it, Dad—you say you're a Christian—what do yours reflect?

"No offense—I love you with all my heart. You know that! But the pattern of your life speaks loud and clear of a faith and trust in something entirely different—a faith and trust in yourself alone. Your life is a monument to what relentless driving human will power, self-reliance, discipline, and great physical energy can sometimes achieve in this world. But, Dad, you've built your life on the sand of your self-centered priorities. Now the rains have fallen—the floods have come, storms blow and your great, tall, glorious monument to yourself has been swept into the sea."

Then Roc shared with me some Scripture and explained how these truths applied to my problem. And as we talked I could feel my perspective changing. I could see some light filtering through the tunnel of my despair. I found I could reason with him—follow his logic, and my bitterness and tension and anxiety and doom began to subside.

My son was helping me become aware that my problem was not a bombing-across-the-border problem, it was a way-of-life problem. Anyway, time was running out, so he pulled it all together into a simple little summary.

"Look, Dad, Jesus Christ made one basic claim. He made it many times in a variety of places, but it was always the same. He claimed to have a Father-Son identity with God, such that all the power of the universe was available to Him—Jesus.

"Now watch this—He also made us one basic promise. He promised you and me that if we would believe what He said, invite Him to come into our lives so that we could live as He taught, He would make that same power available to us.

"Now catch this one, too—Jesus really gave us one basic teaching—and upon this fundamental, He said, hang all the teachings of all the prophets through all the ages: love God with all your heart, with all your soul, with all your mind—and love your neighbor as yourself."

Then we talked about what this teaching, in practice, looks

like in a person's life-style. In other words, how a man or woman lives if he really loves the Lord, and if he really loves his neighbor as himself. This means that all a man's resources are equally available to his neighbor as they are available to himself—his love, his time, his talents, his concern, his tools, his money, his ideas, his labor—he lives an incredibly different life. And his neighbor is every other living human being who needs something he has to share.

Well, we agreed, that would be some exciting way of life. Then Roc continued: "Now hear this last link in the chain: Jesus Christ came on earth—walked into human history—for one basic reason. He came to guide man back to God. You see, man, filled with pride and misled by visions of his own power and importance, deliberately turned away from God to make his own rules, his own plans and to go his own way. This grieved God deeply just as a parent is grieved when a child runs away from home.

"Yet God loved His children so completely that He chose to send His only Son to live as a human being, and to reestablish contact with men's hearts and minds and to pay the ransom for man's desertion. The penalty for desertion—the basic sin—is death. So His Son, Jesus, laid down His life on the cross in our place and thus cleared the way for all of us to be forgiven, so that we can return, without fear of punishment to the loving companionship with God, as it was intended in the beginning. Having done that for us, He rose victorious over death and is here now, ready to lead us back to God and to the abundant life that His fellowship brings—if by our own free will we choose to go."

In this vein, we talked and exchanged views for an hour. And the more we talked, the more I felt the grip and twist of tension and guilt in my gut and brain begin to relax and dissipate. I spoke out of my new feeling, "Son, I think I understand what you are saying. As I see it now, I've made one major strategic mistake in my life. It wasn't the pioneer philosophy of my father. It wasn't the sophisticated metaphysics of my West Point years.

"I deliberately selected to live my life *alone*. But you have convinced me that God never intended man to do it alone. He created man to dream and build and conquer and explore together with Him—in fellowship, in companionship.

"Ya' know, if I ever get the opportunity to build again in this life, I hope I don't make these mistakes again. I had built my life on the sand of man-centered appetites and goals and human willpower. Then came the storm of crisis, and all I built was swept away.

"I hope I never try again to do it all alone, but rather align myself with the power that controls the universe, for He holds the reins of the galaxies in His hands. If I'm with Him, I'll never be concerned about control."

My son broke in, "Dad, you are depicting the kind of building that Jesus was describing to all of us in the third chapter of the Revelation when He said, 'Behold, I stand at the door and knock. If anyone hears my knock and opens the door, I will come in to him'—and together we will build him a life on solid rock. It will be life so much more meaningful, so much more powerful, so much more significant than anything he ever dreamed was possible, that he won't even remember his former groping and struggling for meaning in life."

My mind raced. I could almost visualize this new life. I said, "That's the desire of my heart. This shattering experience has demonstrated to me how fragile is fame, and how fleeting, power; how empty of real meaning is the vicious, killing scramble up life's mountain just because it's there. My world—my career—my life has been demolished.

"Now I want whatever years remain to me to have significance—however small—but eternal meaning in the eyes of God and my fellowmen. Before He struck me to my knees, I had felt His presence and turned away. Then I sensed His absence; I knew He was right outside the door of my life, but I scoffed Him off.

"Tell me, how does a man negotiate that curious metaphor of 'opening the door'?"

My son spoke quietly and deliberately. "Dad, there are probably hundreds of ways that door can be opened. But all of them have one thing in common. You have to do it of your own free will. When you are really in earnest that you want to turn your life around and walk the rest of your life on earth and forever more with the living God, you open the door by opening communication with Him in utter sincerity and faith and tell Him that you have made that decision. And He has promised that He will come into your life and guide you to an eternity of real significance and abundance. . . ."

I cut him off. "Show me how."

It was dark now in the jungle. And 15,000 miles away in Lafayette, Indiana, it was past midnight. Yet I felt as though we were side-by-side in the same room, as my son and I knelt down together and opened the door. We opened communication with the living God.

It was so simple, so direct, so straight and clean and open. We just prayed together: "Lord Jesus, I need You. I open the door of my life and welcome You in as my Saviour and Lord. Thank You for forgiving my sins. I have some idea of what that cost You. Please take control of my life and make me the sort of man You want me to be."

There was a pause. Then my son let out a shout that must

have been heard all over the state of Indiana. It was a shout of pure joy.

For Roc, this was a direct answer to prayer. Four years, every night, he had prayed for my salvation—prayed that somehow, somewhere, sometime, I would be brought to my knees and find cause to pause and open the door to Jesus Christ.

Now it had happened. And Roc could hardly believe it. For, in the middle of an ordinary night, God had rewarded his persistent faith and brought his prodigal father home.

11
on fire!

Our hour on the MARS radio-telephone network was up. Roc assigned me some homework to do, and we said good night. All around my little hooch was a warm, golden glow. It felt like morning, yet it was really just drawing night. But to me it was dawn—dawn of the first day of the rest of my life.

Without removing boots or flying suit, I flopped onto the bed and slept the peace that usually only tiny children know. Morning found me at the chapel door. I was embarrassed. I had to ask to borrow a Bible—more humiliating, I had to ask for help in finding some of the passages my son had assigned. I had thought Deuteronomy was one of those two-humped camels that the wise men rode from the east.

Hours flew by as I read and prayed and walked apart and reflected on the beautiful conversation I had had with my son. I could feel the warm breath of the Spirit of God blow through me, sweep me out, clean me out and throw out junk I'd been collecting for 50 years.

Two days later, my general, "The Boss," flew in. I wasn't afraid now. I escorted him in, and he sat in the big, red leather chair in my office. I stood at attention opposite. In his quiet, but direct, low key voice, looking me straight in the eye, he expressed his disappointment that a fellow West Pointer whom he had handpicked to command his greatest fighter wing—just because one of his buddies was shot out of the sky at his side—would lose his temper and declare his own war, by his own rules. Then he reached into his pocket and drew out a folded yellow sheet of paper—covered with teletype. He slapped it on the desk between us, turning it for me to read.

It was a message from the Joint Chiefs of Staff to the Theater Commander. In all capital letters it read:

NEW RULE OF ENGAGEMENT—REPEAT—NEW RULE OF ENGAGEMENT. BECAUSE OF THE NUMEROUS VIOLATIONS BY THE ENEMY OF OUR NO BOMBING—NO FIRING AGREEMENT. EFFECTIVE THIS DATE AND TIME IF THEY FIRE ACROSS THE BORDER AT ANY OF YOUR AIRCRAFT, YOU ARE AUTHORIZED TO RETALIATE.

The general's thumb was covering up the date-time sequence which made the message effective—and this was rather important to me. I waited a moment in spastic anticipation. My head rang. The muscles on my neck and shoulders clutched and unclutched. Impulsively I reached out and swept his hand away!

The effective date was the day *before* I had bombed in North Vietnam.

I heaved a sigh of relief that was heard all the way to Bangkok. Spontaneously, I burst out, "Chief! I've been saved again by my lucky stars!"

The general gave me one of those level, nothing looks, picked up his hat, slapped it on his thigh and walked to the door. As he gripped the brass knob, he turned back and, pointing at me, shook his head slowly. "This was not luck, my friend. You were saved by the grace of God, and don't you ever forget that."

I listened to the echo of his footfalls receding down the hall and heard the guard at the door call, "Attention."

Then he was gone. I moved slowly to the window and watched his jet gather speed as it lifted off into the monsoon mist. "There goes a real king," I said to myself, "and his heart is in the hands of the Lord." I felt a warmth for that man that I had never felt before toward a man of authority.

As the days walked by, and I found I could trust God's promises, I began to turn more and more of my life over to His influence. Everyone around me began to see that something significant had happened to me. My life had definitely turned a corner.

One day as I was leaving the mess hall, two of my pilots pulled me aside. "Colonel, normally we wouldn't try you with something like this."

"Try me." I smiled.

"We've been working with the kids in the village. Have you seen their school? They don't even have a place to get together all at once. When the teachers want to assemble the group they have to meet in the muddy field outside.

"In the monsoon, the place is a mire. In the dry season, it's too hot to breathe. They need an auditorium—and we have that great pile of lumber in supply."

"Hold it, guys," I cut in. "That lumber is for a contingency. A tornado might wipe us out."

The captain was very respectful. "Sir, there hasn't been a tornado in this valley since the Great Khan invaded."

The next week work began on the new multi-purpose auditorium in the village of Takhli. And with it a new sparkle in the eyes of mothers, teachers and children.

A week or so later, my redheaded flight surgeon asked me to jeep into town with him one night. It was his weekly inspection of the local honky-tonks. But that wasn't his real mission this time. He couldn't wait to let me know that everyone had noticed a major change in my attitude. He broached a subject.

The little village of Nakhon Sawan, twenty miles up the river, was infested with a tropical disease that was eating away at the eyelids and lips of the children. The village doctor was unable to cope with the epidemic. But we had two tropical disease specialists who wanted to go help. If we could send a mobile dispensary to hold clinic twice a week, he was confident it would help the village, advance the experience of the doctors and do marvels for community relations.

I hedged. Could we afford this new program? He looked me right in the eye and almost knocked a wooden-wheeled hay cart off the road.

"Chief, the word is around that you've become a Christian. Welcome to the club. God will surely provide the resources if we provide the concern."

Within a month the epidemic was arrested. Not long ago I got a letter from one of my old combat companions who had stayed on in Thailand as a civilian employee after the base at Takhli was closed. He warmed my heart with the news that our little dispensary had grown into a twenty-four-bed hospital—still flagged by the original sign out front:

```
GI HOSPITAL

GOD LOVES BUDDHISTS TOO

COME AND BE HEALED
```

The days rolled by, and I was shortly visited by one of my favorite generals from our administrative headquarters in the Philippines, Lieutenant General Francis P. Gideon. We had a warm time together because we had been old tennis antagonists over the years. As we sat in my staff car beside his airplane saying good-bye he confided what I already knew in my heart. My chances for promotion had probably gone down the drain with my impulsive, undisciplined air strike on the border. A technicality had saved me legally and, although my long excellent record had spared me the very harsh punishment that normally would have accompanied a breach of air discipline, my credibility as a totally reliable leader worthy of general officer rank had been demolished.

I was surprised that this realization had very little impact on me. Of far more significance was whether I would be allowed to fly and fight again, not by temporal authority, for I already knew I was released by my Air Force bosses to resume my appointed tasks in the air and on the ground. Nevertheless, I was in prayer daily, seeking God's direction. Did He mean for me to bomb again?

I felt during those fresh new days as a baby Christian such a completely direct and uncomplicated relationship with God, I identified completely with the original disciples at Pentecost. I wanted desperately to take exactly the steps He wanted me to take—all of them, but only them. I did not want to fall off one inch. I knew I had not yet turned all of my life over to Him, but I was sure that I would as we moved ahead together, and I learned to trust Him completely.

I read Paul's letter to the Romans and was, of course, completely in accord with his clear instructions: "Let every person be subject to the governing authorities. For there is no authority except from God, and those that exist have been initiated by God" (Rom. 13:1, *RSV*). That was so directly in line with my training, it was easy to grasp.

But contrarily, I could not turn away from Jesus' simple and direct command in Matthew 5: "You have heard that it was said, 'You shall love your neighbor, and hate your enemy! But I say to you, love your enemies . . ." (Matt. 5:43,44, *RSV*). How could I love my enemy and go out to kill him?

My immature faith led me to seek advice from more mature Christians. I addressed my problem to my favorite chaplain. He was not sure of the answer. He tended to feel that Jesus was not referring to war, but to personal relationships within one's near community. He advised me to go along with Paul.

I chatted with my Base Commander whom I had identified as a mature Christian. He suggested that, while he accepted all Scripture as inspired by God, he felt that some of Paul's letters were directed at specifics. He suggested that Paul was addressing his counsel to Christians in Rome—advising them to not make civil disobedience waves as their efforts would be more fruitful if fitted into the law and order of the time, so as to expand their base and grow strong rather than to risk wipe-out by opposing the power of Roman rule.

I chose to go directly to God in prayer and seek His guiding hand in *my* time—in *my* context specifically. I knew I was that close to Him.

I did not have long to wait. On December 6 my name came up to lead a strike on a military complex in the Bat Lake area—a significant and dangerous mission against a specific priority target in North Vietnam assigned by the Joint Chiefs of Staff.

I wanted to lead the strike badly, but I also was somewhat apprehensive. Bat Lake was a heavily defended enemy supply zone, bristling with guns and missiles. I prayed in the very direct, conversational way that my son had taught me, asking Him to show me how He wanted me to serve Him. I was convinced that, young in Christ though I was, He had clearly promised to listen and respond.

As the sand of the hourglass sifted toward the appointed briefing time, I felt no urge to strike my name from the lineup. The early morning briefing was crisp, cool routine. Everyone knew it was going to be a tough, but exciting adventure.

I relaxed my soul—swung its door wide open and confidently awaited God's hand as I moved through that incredible count-down routine leading up to take-off that only a fighter pilot knows: the fellowship in the equipment room as Sergeant Bowman double-checked my parachute with me; the brotherly super-calm laugh with my black crew chief—a staff sergeant named Willman whom I had learned to love and respect and trust more than anyone else on this earth; the booming engine start; the taxi out.

God had everything going A-Okay: the marshaling, the last check, the take-off and join-up—smooth as silk. God wanted me to go back to war.

I spotted the target on the lake's edge. There were tiny fingers of smoke rising from the enemy camp. The triple canopy of the jungle close up to the lake's edge hid the defending guns as well as the stacked supplies of food, fuel and ammunition—but we knew what they had.

I timed it carefully—we must not circle, but catch them by surprise. I made no radio call; just dipped my wing to signal and dove like a falcon. The altimeter raced. The airspeed bounded.

Suddenly the sky was ablaze with red and white puffs. Antiaircraft fire! Heavy. Close.

I jinked—then steadied my sight on the target. Down—down—down—now! I squeezed the bomb release button and pulled hard, pressing rudder.

"Wham!" Something hit me like a baseball bat. I plunged against the harness and belt. A ball of fire enveloped me. I kicked rudders instinctively.

Escape!

I was hit!

The acrid smell of smoke! Oh, God—on fire!

I stroked the afterburner for more speed. Pow! I hit the back of my seat. My head banged the canopy.

My eyes cleared. I glanced up—and saw the whirling jungle overhead. I was inverted, but rolling and diving. The airspeed raced—600—650—black smoke now enveloped my canopy.

"Lead, you're hit. Head east for the gulf." Someone back in the flight had noticed my plight and called advice on the radio.

Now at the speed of sound I regained control but was headed west—dodging—ducking—out of the target area. It was getting too hot to fly. I pulled back the stick and shot straight up. I needed altitude to punch out.

I prayed: "God, I gave You command of my life and I know You are in control. But I also know I am in serious trouble, so here I come. When I get as close to heaven as this horse will go—either that fire goes out or I go out."

Up—up—up, I shot past 5,000—10,000—20,000. The air thinned out. The airspeed bled off 600—500—300—100—000.

For a timeless moment we stopped dead in space . . . pointing to heaven.

Then like a spent arrow, that great steel knife dropped straight back, plunging toward earth in a screaming reverse dive. Slowly at first—then faster, faster, faster—down, down, down—tail first. I tried to move the stick, but it was frozen stiff. I kicked the rudders for my life.

I slammed the throttle full open—nothing! Flamed out!

At 10,000 feet I grabbed both ejection handles, but the negative Gs against the shoulder harness cut off my arm leverage. I couldn't pull.

5,000 . . . 4,000. . . .

"Lord, I need You now. I'm out of altitude, out of power and out of control. I claim Your promise to never leave me nor forsake me."

Suddenly the dense atmosphere caught the controls and washed us out into a great, rearward, scything arc across the sky. Like a giant pendulum, my steel bird sailed slowly backward and upward to a stop . . . paused . . . and then dove in a long, steep glide toward earth. I pressed the air start button, heard the engine rumble to life and felt a surge of power!

Hallelujah! Just as the jagged mountain cliffs reached up for me, God caught that steel Frisbee just off the canyon floor and sailed it back into the sky.

The fire was out and I was on my way home.

My general's voice on the phone was, as always, cool, low key, imperative. "Beautiful job, Bo. The complex was completely destroyed. No friendly losses.

"God is talking to you; pay attention."

11
it's got to be a miracle

The months flew by and soon I was on my way home. My three years of combat in Southeast Asia were over. I was assigned to Norton Air Force Base at San Bernardino, California.

My family meanwhile was scattered all over the national landscape. The youngsters—typical youth of the 1960s—were wandering, experimenting, searching for meaning. My wife, Betty, was doing her own thing in real estate in Arlington, Virginia. We had all fallen pretty much out of touch and hadn't corresponded regularly for three or four years.

The general feeling in the family was that I had deserted

them to live my own private adventure, to achieve my own career goals. Still, when the word reached them through the Air Force grapevine that the legendary warlord was finally returning to his fatherland, they all gathered at my new base of assignment. Why they came, I didn't know at the time. Morbid curiosity, I guessed. Perhaps they were curious as to how the old hero would look after all that time away.

So the family gathered at San Bernardino, having decided that the time was right to make one last effort to bring us all together again. Without knowing where or why, they chose a home right under the eaves of Campus Crusade for Christ headquarters at Arrowhead Springs. Betty had always been a church-going, neighbor-loving person all her life, but never before had she encountered the basic plan of salvation. Now Crusader neighbors Dorothy Mayell, Barbara Fain and Vonette Bright took her under their wing, teaching her the simple truth of the gospel—salvation by faith in Jesus Christ alone. And they won her with the same overpowering love with which my son had first brought these same truths home to me.

The chain reaction of God's love which Roc had set in motion in our family continued working unabated. Our daughter Viki came up from the Caribbean and spent a week with Roc in Valdosta, Georgia where he was busy training young pilots at Moody Air Force Base. While she was there, he led her to the Lord.

Viki came home really on fire and Spirit-filled and enlisted as a volunteer secretary in Campus Crusade's Military Ministry. She was soon joined there by Beverly Gaylord, the first full-time staff woman in the Military Ministry. Beverly moved into our home and soon was discipling our other daughters, Sheri and Kris.

About this same time, my other son, Kirk—who also had been led to Christ by Roc—became involved in Campus Crusade's Student Life program in Pacific High School. Kirk, his buddy Kirk Pagel and his sister Sheri took over leadership of the backyard evangelism meetings of the High School Ministry.

Suddenly, our family was on fire for the Lord in all directions. That is, all our family except me. And what was wrong with me? I was having trouble growing. I had accepted Jesus Christ in Thailand and had been powerfully aglow. But as the months passed without a big brother in Christ to push me and guide me, the fire cooled down to an ember. My daily Bible study fell before the pressure of work and my once close walk with God became a somewhat distant faith. Moreover, I began falling back into my old carnal habits.

Christmas, 1971 arrived and with it God sent Roc home on leave. He noticed my problem at once. First of all, he set the family into a routine of Bible study and morning devotions that established us—both as individual Christians and as a unit—in a more disciplined way of life. Then he talked to me about my problem. He earnestly impressed upon me the high-priority need of finding a big brother in Christ who would lead me in growth and maturity.

Just as Betty had found a spiritual big sister in Dorothy Mayell, so I found a wonderful big brother in her husband and Viki's boss, Lionel Mayell, of the Military Ministry office at Arrowhead Springs. For four years Lionel has chipped away at this rough, tough diamond. He has almost taught me how to love.

From the beginning, Lionel took me with him everywhere. He taught me how to pray. He taught me how to testify. And he taught me how to study the Bible. But even more than that, he also taught me how to believe the Bible—for he recognized that I was still skeptical about much that I studied in God's Word.

One day he got me aside in his car. "Look, Colonel, you can't expect to build a belief on air. You've got to lay a scriptural foundation for your faith. You do this by reading God's Word—the Bible. And I mean seriously *read* it and *study* it and *memorize* it.

"Now I know you have reservations about some portions of this Book. But you're not alone. Every intelligent believer has had these same intellectual problems at one time or another. Perhaps it would help you to know how most of them have hurdled this same obstacle.

"First, you've got to read the Word with an open heart— searching for truth and meaning. But try to relax and listen to God talk—don't fight the Word. Then discuss your readings with mature Christian friends. Finally, think and pray about issues as they arise in your heart.

"This process leads you ultimately to an understanding, appreciation and belief in the main message of the book. But there will remain still in the back of your mind a residue of partially resolved discrepancies, unexplained contradictions and other apparent deficiencies which something inside you will not allow you to accept totally, such as the accounts of Creation perhaps, or maybe the Great Flood or the sun standing still. . . .

"Why is this?

"Here's why. The eyes with which you see and the mind with which you reason are conditioned to a natural, physical world. Contrarily, in the Bible, God is dealing often with spiritual, supernatural phenomena. Obviously, when you try to evaluate or interpret the supernatural while employing natural reference points, your mind predictably rejects the thought. It says, 'Wait a minute, something's wrong. This doesn't make sense.'

"So what do you do? . . .

"Colonel, every Christian sometime has had to pile up his own little collection of skepticisms, then dig a pit in his own path and dump them all in, every one. After that, he has had to take a running jump across that pit—and never look back. This is his *personal leap of faith.*

"Now you've reached that point in your path. Dig a pit in it and unload in it everything you're skeptical about. Take your own personal leap of faith across it. Then keep going and don't look back.

"As you grow and mature as a Christian, the Holy Spirit will resolve these doubts one by one. And in later years when you happen to pass this way again, you'll be surprised to find that the pit has somehow filled itself in. The hangups have disappeared, and you can walk that path with your eyes closed because He has you by the hand."

I don't recall ever seeing a Bible open or hearing a prayer spoken in my home before I went away to war. Now every morning of our lives when the family is together, we open the day with Him. We call it, "First Hour with God."

We gather together in a family circle before breakfast around the fireside or, in summer, out under the redwoods. We sing a song of joy together. We read aloud a couple of chapters of Scripture. We discuss their meaning and beauty. Then we pray out loud, handing it off from one to another around the circle.

We thank God for what He has done in our lives individually, changing us so completely by giving each one new beauty and direction and meaning. And we thank God for what he has done for us as a family, taking a scattering of spiritual nomads and bringing us together into a devoted, loving, dedicated American family. Then we thank God in advance for what He is going to do with us as we walk out into the day, sharing with others this love and this faith that now binds us to Him and to one another.

I find it incredible, almost impossible to comprehend the tremendous power, the volume, the quality of God's love: a love He has showered down upon my family, not because we deserve it—because we don't, but just because He loves us. Just because He is totally interested in and concerned about each one of us individually. Our ultimate growth and flowering to beauty, our eternal welfare are important to Him—no matter how inconsequential we may feel ourselves to be.

How do I know God is concerned about each of us? Because He was concerned about me when He saw me, His enemy, charging and fighting my way through life—determined to do it with my own will power, laughing and scoffing at Him, teaching my own children that there was no God. Yet, in the face of all this, He reached down in love, tearing the chains and shackles from my wrists and ankles, and set me free.

He set me free from my blind stampede for power and glory. He opened my eyes and let me see and share in the real way—the real truth—the only life that is eternally significant. He wiped clean my record of 50 years of selfishness, arrogance and belligerence.

Moreover, God has made a place in His own house for Betty and me and all our loved ones to go when our course on earth is run—a place where we can serve Him with exciting, meaningful missions and tasks and adventures forevermore.

Man, that's *love*.

Anyone who knew us before—and knows us now—would surely agree that what God has done in our family has got to be a miracle. There is no other way to explain it. And day by day, we have learned to expect miracles, day by day.

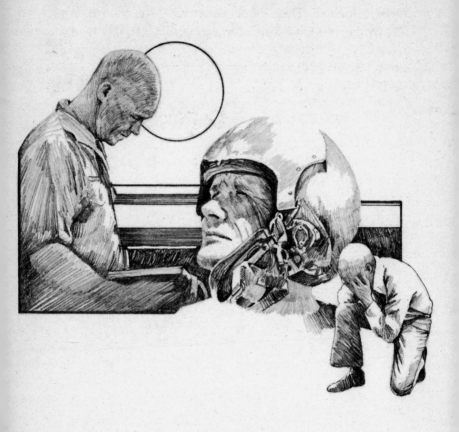

that's
a promise

I am always warmed when I share this story of my life with high school and college students. They come in clusters and say to me, "I recognize the old you. I've known you all my life. You're *my* dad."

This seems to tell me that all the tough, stubborn, power-seeking "fighter pilots" in this world are not necessarily Air Force colonels. We are part of every walk of life. We are in commerce, in business, in industry, in the Mafia, in religion, in education, in sports. And we are all of one piece—rugged individualists.

Yet—as my son recently confided in me, "Dad, you have proven that God can get into any man's heart. If it could happen to you, there is hope for everyone."

Now hear this also. You might be surprised how my life-style change has penetrated my Air Force associations. Of course, as a Christian, I feel an inner urge to go about talking to young pilots, non-coms and groups of airmen—even generals—about Christ. And I've been encouraged to do this by important government people; for many of our military and civilian leaders appreciate that Christians in key positions at all levels provide the greatest force alive today for halting the moral crumbling, the permissive decay that is destroying our country.

Again and again, I hear general officers, cabinet ministers and congressmen suggesting in quiet earnestness that the days of Solomon have now come to America, that God is calling out once again: "If my people, who are called by my name will realize their sickness and will humble themselves and turn from their wicked ways and seek my face and pray; then I in heaven will hear them, and will forgive their sins and will heal their land" (2 Chron. 7:14, paraphrase).

One of the greatest men of our times recently leaned over a coffee table in his study in Washington, D.C. and carefully, quietly spoke the most perceptive and exciting bit of wisdom I have heard in my lifetime:

"How improbable that the top leadership of the greatest nation in history should suddenly be swept away—President, Vice President, top cabinet ministers, congressional leaders. How seemingly unusual that roughly within the year that same great nation would be defeated and humiliated in a war of wills by a tiny, primitive country of largely poor, barefooted, rice farmers.

"This combination of devastating events can only be the

hand of God reaching again into history as He did long ago. This cannot help but get our attention.

"It cannot help but communicate to every sensible person that the living God is fed up with our moral sickness, our permissive decay, our rejection of Him, and He is signaling us that if we, His people whom He has so richly blessed, do not right now acknowledge our desertion from Him and turn from our wicked ways and seek His face and pray—individually and collectively by the hundreds of thousands—our land will never be healed, but rather will be smashed into oblivion as was Nineveh and Babylon.

"But God loves us and He yearns for us to hear and turn and be healed. And here in Washington, the capital of our land, I feel it beginning. Everywhere I look men are praying again. Thank God!"

Now, let me get very personal. If you do not have a close, personal relationship with Jesus Christ, you are wasting your life. You may think your life is a grand success, Or, contrarily, you may feel that you deserve a more abundant, more meaningful life.

Think it over. What does your walk on this earth really mean? What eternal significance lies in your years of toil? What will happen when you're through? Will you only be dumped back in the earth and become dust? Or will you live on forever, exploring and developing the universe with God?

Perhaps you, as I once did, sometimes pause and notice that unexplainable, hollow, God-shaped vacuum within your being. Perhaps you too have heard that faint knock that tells you God is right outside, waiting and wanting to come in and set your soul at peace, to join with you in a life of real abundance, real importance, real meaning.

Why don't you open the door of your heart and life to Him? Go to Him in prayer—simple, sincere, direct prayer. Your words are as good as mine. It's the attitude that counts.

I know for sure that God listens to such prayers as this:

"Lord Jesus, I need You. I open the door of my life and welcome You in as my Saviour and Lord. Thank You for forgiving my sins. Now take control of my life and make me the sort of person You want me to be."

Now—once you've done that—stand back and enjoy the action. Expect miracles, because a whole new life will surely follow your decision to follow Him.

That's a promise!

Not mine—His.

epilogue

A certain man had two sons, and he gathered them together one day, saying, "Boys, I have given you a solid birthright and a sound start in life. Like my father before me, I have taught you the great values of developing independence and self-reliance, the overcoming force of persistence and determination, the power of the human will, and the greatest truth of all—to thine own self be true.

"Now I have many talents which are not being put to use in this mean, routine, structured prison of a life. I must go abroad in the world before I am old. I must explore and adventure and multiply my talents that my days on earth be not wasted."

The two sons agreed each in his own heart that he had indeed fallen heir to an abundant birthright, had been counseled well through his formative years and needed no longer a father to discipline and guide his footsteps.

Not many days after that, the man gathered all his talents together and took a journey into a far country. There he wasted his talents one after another, stubbornly and vainly pursuing a phantom of power and glory as a fighter pilot. Through wind and rain, through desert and jungle, across mountains and skies, amid heat and thirst, sickness and pain, he flew in vain pursuit of the elusive shade.

Finally, one glorious day, in joy and exultation, he cornered the ghostly delusion on a bright, high crag in the clouds. He made one final brash leap to grasp, to hold and not to yield. But the phantom faded and the valiant fighter fell, and great was the fall of him.

Down . . . down . . . he fell. He lost his power; he lost his strength; he lost his influence; he lost his pride. Into the valley of the shadow, he tumbled and rolled.

There, broken and wounded, he wandered and stumbled. For three days and nights, he groped and wept and sank down in the shadow of Satan's massive dungeon. Exhausted, hungry, bleeding and afraid, he wanted gladly to scrub the dungeon floors for one faint glimmer of hope that he might be found and saved and freed from this endless, hopeless maze.

At dusk on the third day, broken and dying on the cold stone floor of the chasm, the old warrior heard a sound in the distance, a knocking on the door of the valley. He called out in the darkness for help. Down the pathway out of the light came his two sons.

While still a great way off, they had heard of their missing father's plight and had flown to find him and to help him. They found the mountains and they found the valley of the shadow; they heard his call and shouted back, and they ran to him and picked him up and carried him home.

His wife and daughters saw them coming far off and ran toward them crying with joy. They fell on one another's necks and kissed and rejoiced. His wife called out to the children, "Hurry, fetch his old West Point bathrobe and put it on him. Put a new ribbon on his chest and new boots on his feet. And put the turkey in the oven and pour some wine.

"Let us feast and be merry. For this is your father, my husband, our pilot. He was dead and is alive again; he was lost and is found."